THE BiG easy BOOK OF Rock Guitar

easy GUITAR TAB EDITION

P9-DZM-307

58 SONGS
42 LEGENDARY ARTISTS!

Company | Gnarls Barkley | Jackson Browne | Buckcherry | Chevelle | vis Costello | Cream | Creed | Sheryl Crow | Gavin DeGraw | The Doobi | ce | Finger Eleven | Grateful Dead | Green Day | Guns N' Roses | Hoob | ckson | Journey | Avril Lavigne | Led Zeppelin | The Motels | Nickelba | Pink Floyd | The Pretenders | Radiohead | Ramones | R.E.M. | The Ro | ntana | Santana featuring Rob Thomas | Seether featuring Amy Lee | y and the Family Stone | Staind | Three Dog Night | Trapt | Van Halen

Alfred Publishing Co., Inc.
16320 Roscoe Blvd., Suite 100
P.O. Box 10003
Van Nuys, CA 91410-0003

alfred.com

ISBN-10: 0-7390-5675-1
ISBN-13: 978-0-7390-5675-2

Cover Photo: STARGAZER TSH-1 courtesy of Schecter Guitar Research

CONTENTS

ARTIST INDEX

ALL I WANNA DO

Words and Music by
SHERYL CROW, WYN COOPER, BILL BOTTRELL,
DAVID FRANCIS BAERWALD and KEVIN GILBERT

Verse 2:
I like a good beer buzz early in the morning,
And Billy likes to peel the labels,
From his bottles of Bud
And shreds them on the bar.
Then he lights every match in an oversized pack;
Letting each one burn down to his thick fingers
Before blowing and cursing them out.
And he's watching the bottles of Bud as they
Spin on the floor.

Pre-chorus 2:
And a happy couple enters the bar dangerously close to one another.
The bartender looks up from his want ads.
(To Chorus:)

Pre-chorus 3:
But otherwise the bar is ours, the day and the night and the car wash too.
The matches and the Buds, and the clean and dirty cars, the sun and the moon.
(To Chorus:)

AMERICAN IDIOT

Words by BILLIE JOE
Music by GREEN DAY

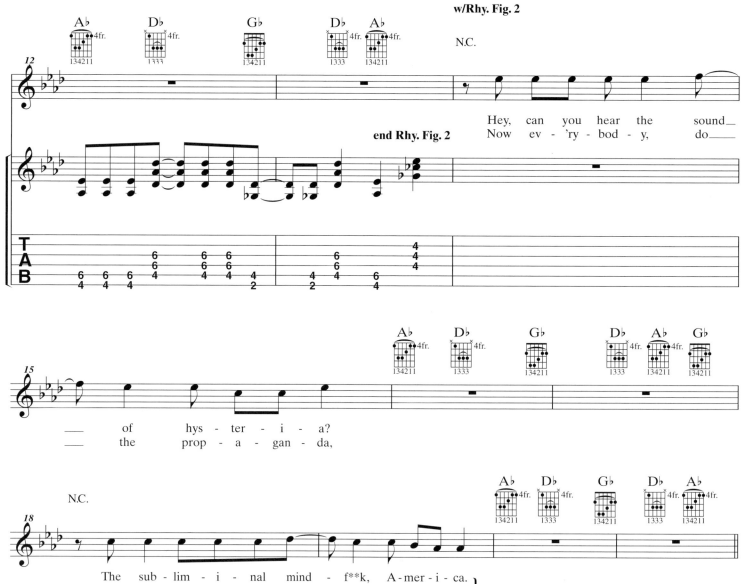

Don't want a na - tion un - der_____ the new me - di - a.
I'm not a part of a red - neck a - gen - da.

w/Rhy. Fig. 2

end Rhy. Fig. 2

Hey, can you hear the sound___
Now ev - 'ry - bod - y, do___

___ of hys - ter - i - a?
___ the prop - a - gan - da,

N.C.

The sub - lim - i - nal mind - f**k, A - mer - i - ca.
and sing a - long to the age_____ of par - a - noi - a.

% *Chorus:*

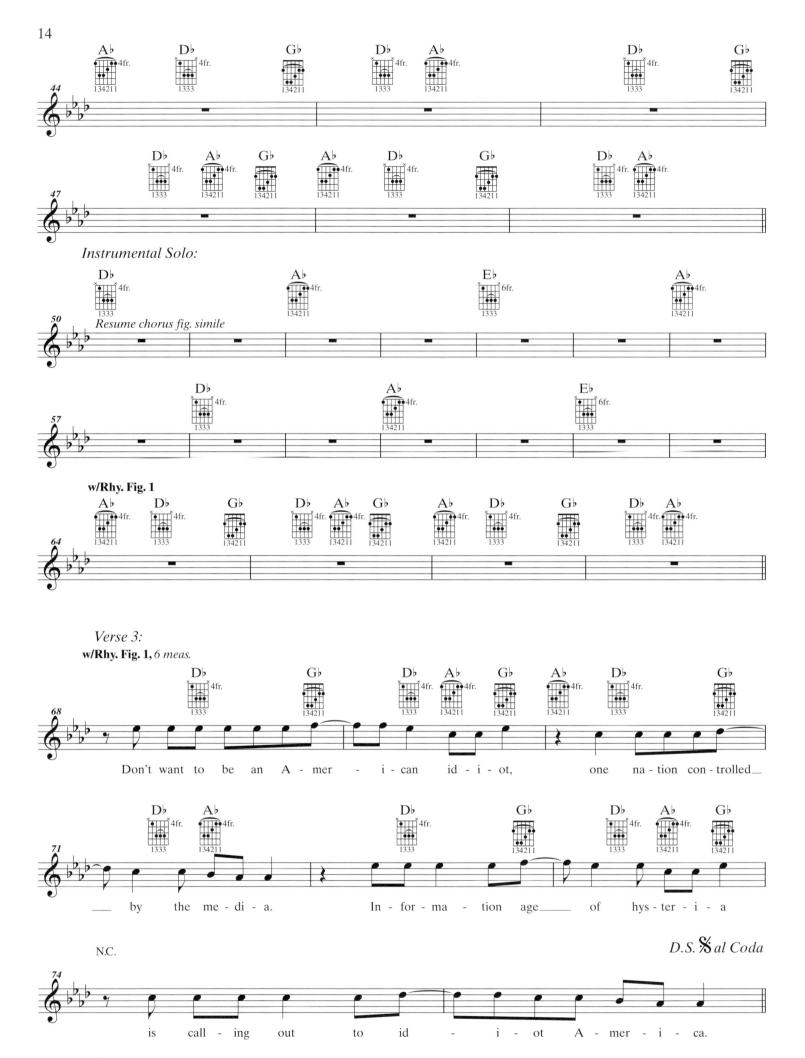

Instrumental Solo:

Resume chorus fig. simile

w/Rhy. Fig. 1

Verse 3:

w/Rhy. Fig. 1, *6 meas.*

Don't want to be an A - mer - i - can id - i - ot, one na - tion con - trolled___

___ by the me - di - a. In - for - ma - tion age___ of hys - ter - i - a

N.C.

D.S. % *al Coda*

is call - ing out to id - i - ot A - mer - i - ca.

Outro:

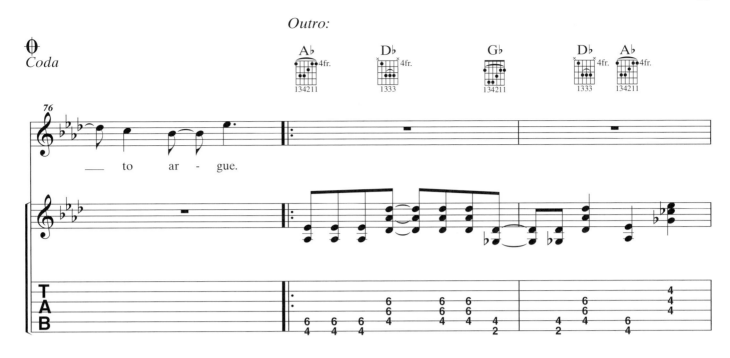

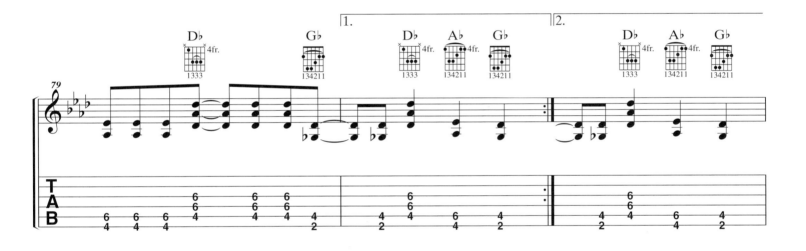

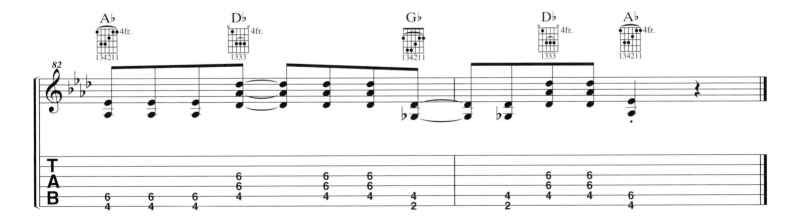

ANOTHER BRICK IN THE WALL

Moderately ♩ = 108

Words and Music by
ROGER WATERS

*2nd time sung by children's chorus 8va.
**Composite arr.

Lyrics:
We don't need no ed-u-ca-tion.

We don't need no thought con-trol. No

dark sar-cas-m in the class-room.

Another Brick in the Wall - 5 - 1

Another Brick in the Wall - 5 - 2

Elec. Gtr. 2 tacet 2 meas.

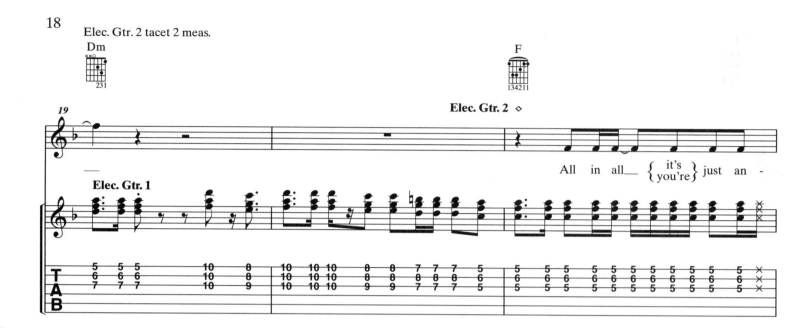

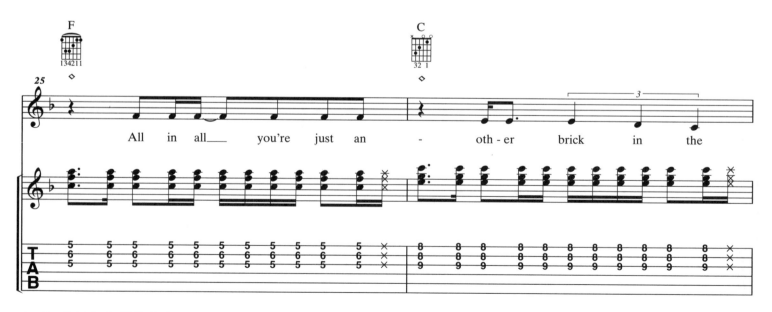

Guitar Solo:
Elec. Gtrs. 1 & 2 tacet

*Chords implied by keyboards.

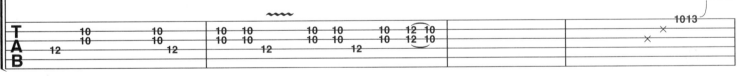

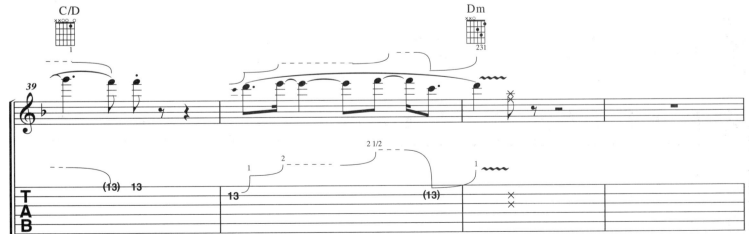

BACK IN BLACK

Words and Music by
ANGUS YOUNG, MALCOLM YOUNG
and BRIAN JOHNSON

Verse:
w/Rhy. Figs. 1 (Elec. Gtr. 1) & 1A (Elec. Gtr. 2) both 2 times

1. Back in   black,_   I hit the sack,   I've been too long, I'm glad_ to be back, yes, I
2. *See additional lyrics
    *Vocal sounds 8va on recording.

Back in Black - 7 - 1

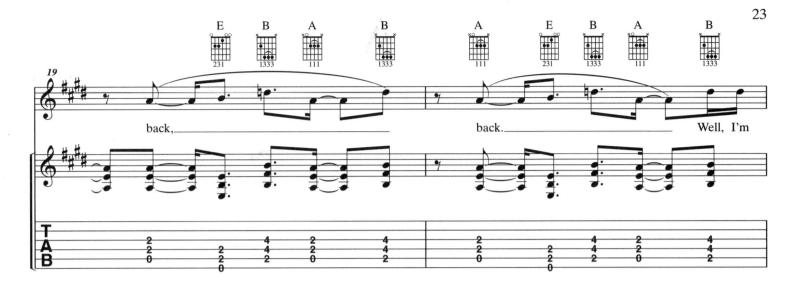

back,_____ back._____ Well, I'm

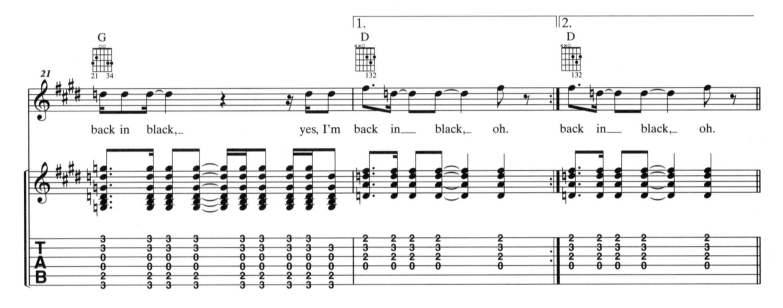

back in black,_ yes, I'm back in_ black,_ oh. back in_ black,_ oh.

Guitar Solo:

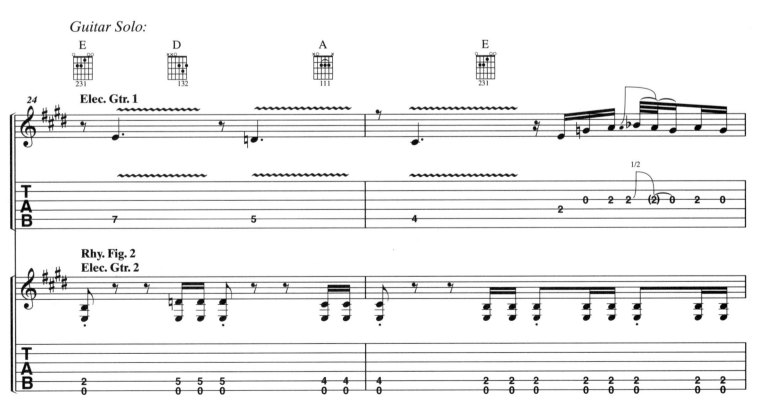

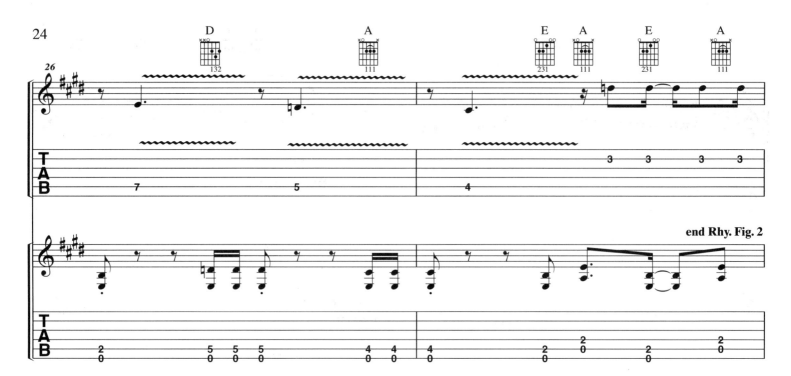

w/**Rhy. Fig. 2** *(Elec. Gtr. 2) 3 times, simile*

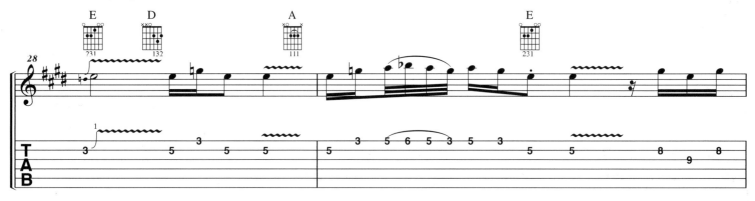

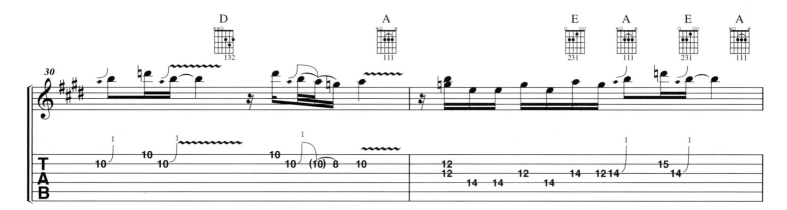

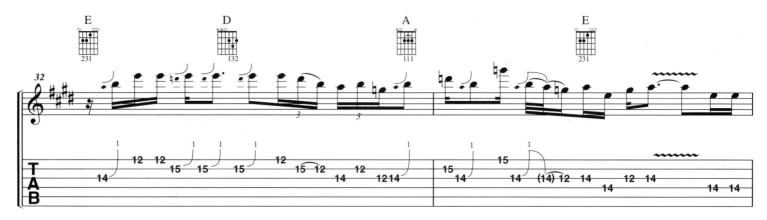

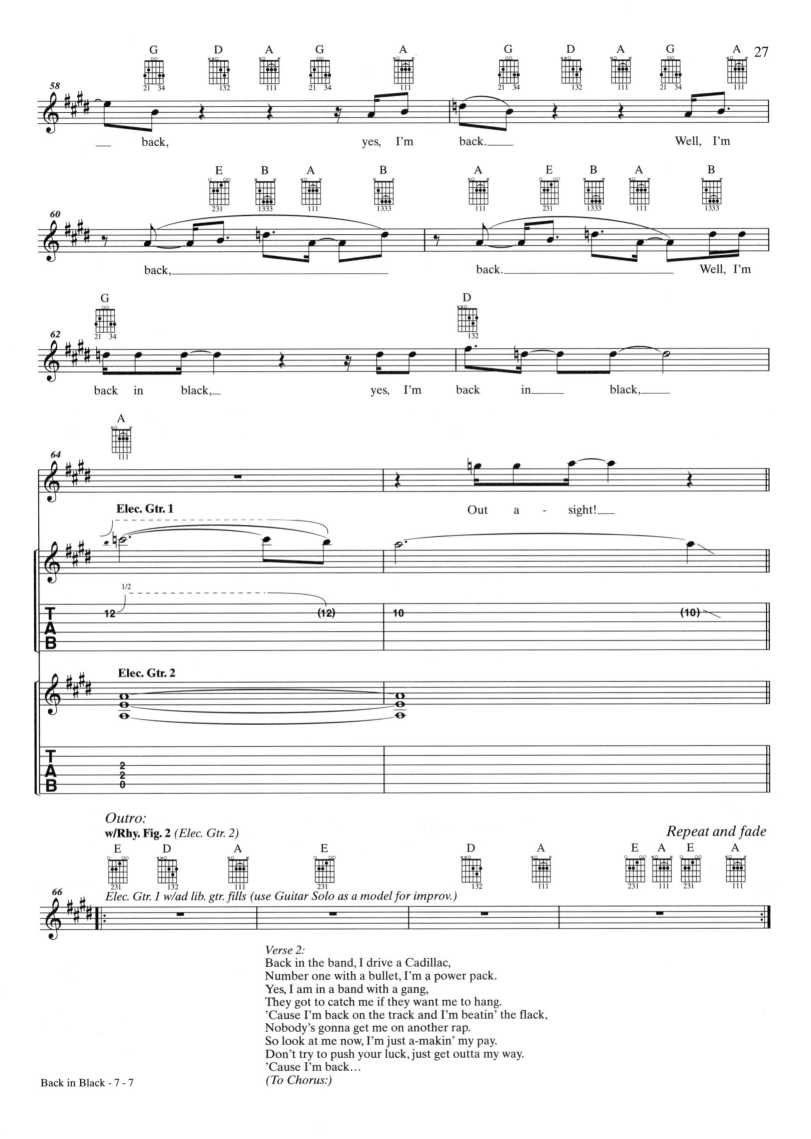

Verse 2:
Back in the band, I drive a Cadillac,
Number one with a bullet, I'm a power pack.
Yes, I am in a band with a gang,
They got to catch me if they want me to hang.
'Cause I'm back on the track and I'm beatin' the flack,
Nobody's gonna get me on another rap.
So look at me now, I'm just a-makin' my pay.
Don't try to push your luck, just get outta my way.
'Cause I'm back…
(To Chorus:)

BASKET CASE

To match record key, tune down 1/2 step

Moderately fast ♩ = 168

Lyrics by BILLIE JOE
Music by GREEN DAY

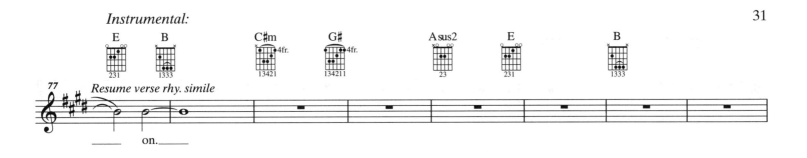

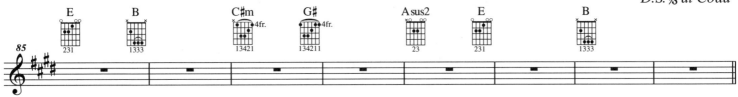

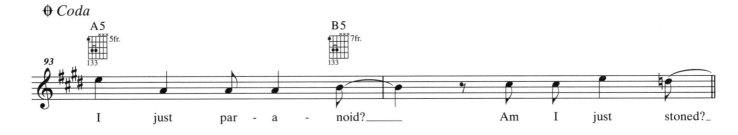

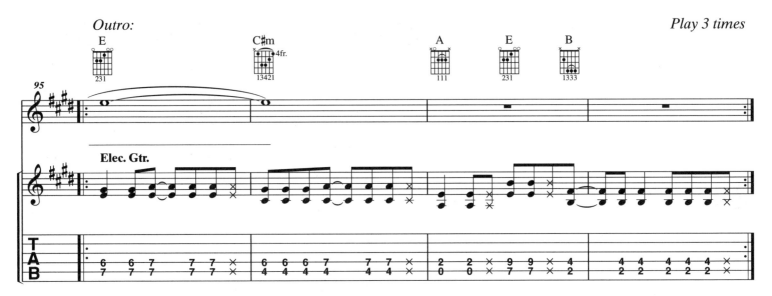

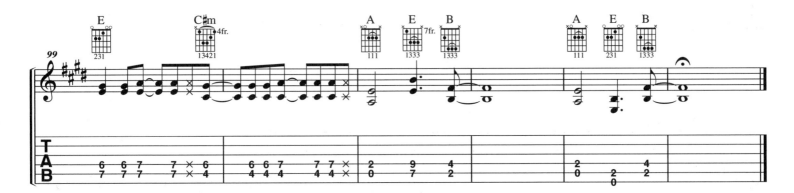

BEAT IT

To match record key, tune down 1/2 step

Written and Composed by
MICHAEL JACKSON

Moderately fast ♩ = 136

Intro:

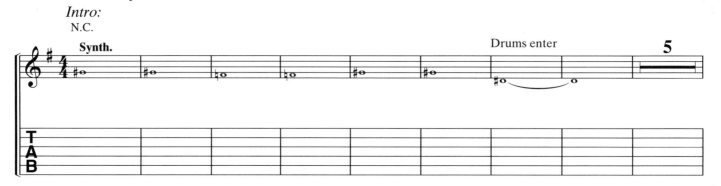

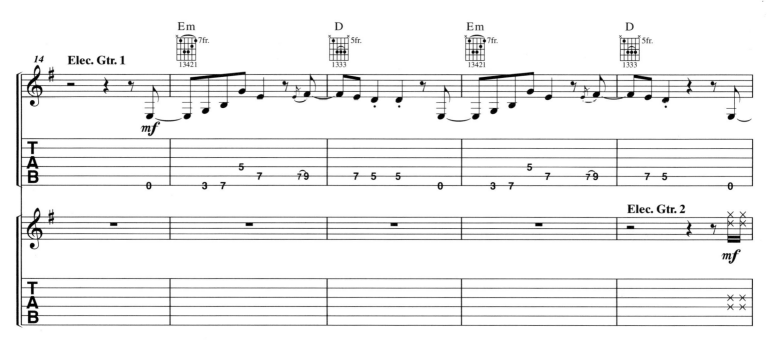

Cont. in slashes

Beat It - 7 - 1

Verse:

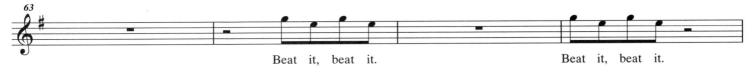

Beat It - 7 - 4

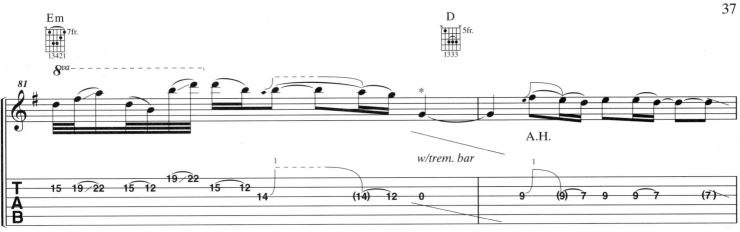

*Depress bar to slack.

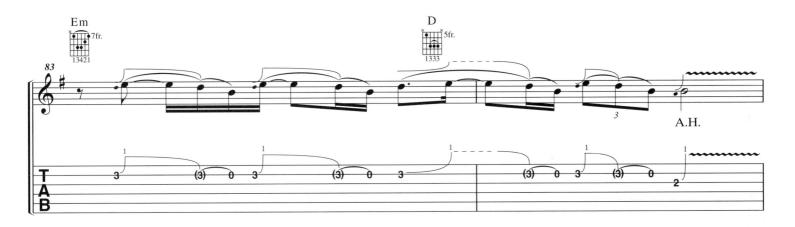

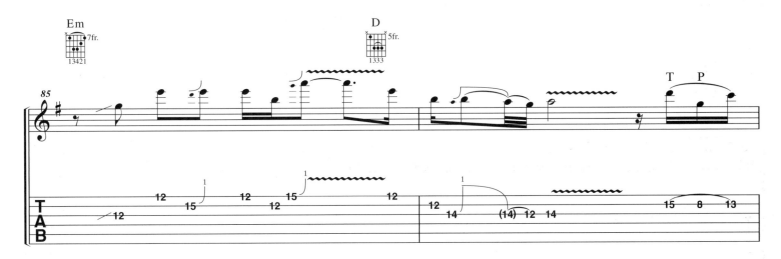

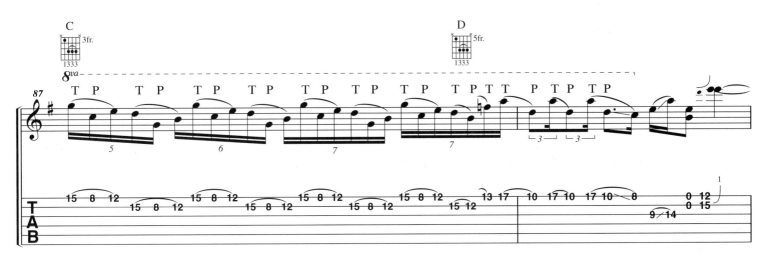

Beat It - 7 - 6

38

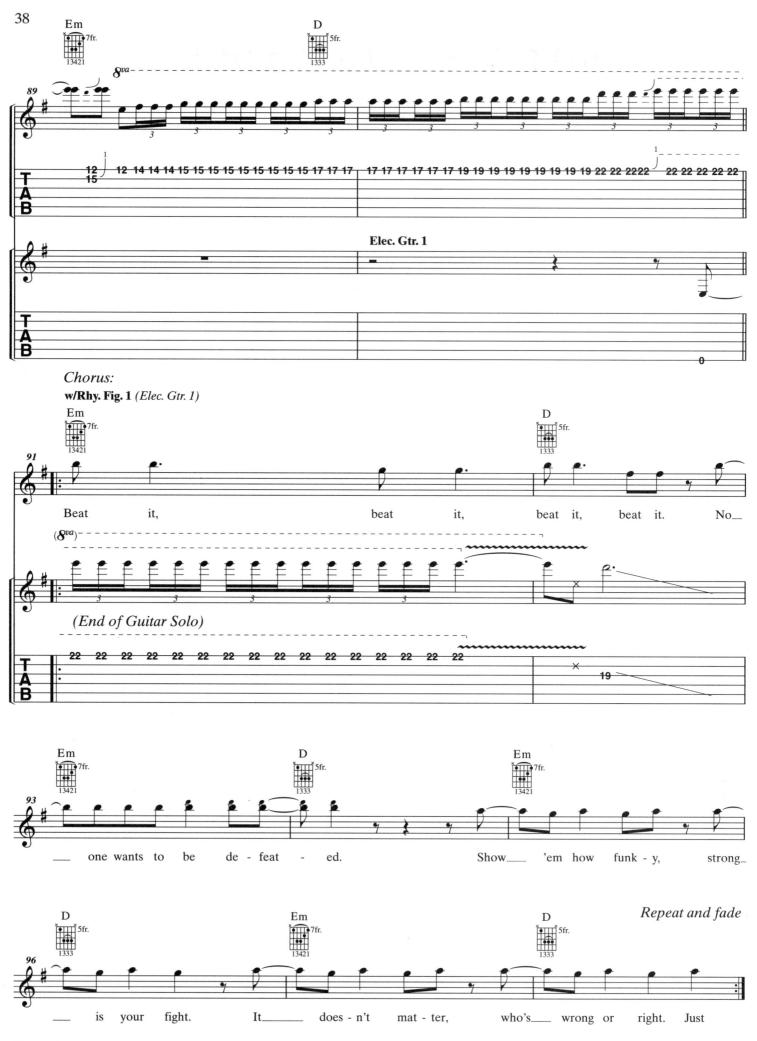

BITTERSWEET SYMPHONY

Written by
MICK JAGGER and KEITH RICHARDS
Lyrics by
RICHARD ASHCROFT

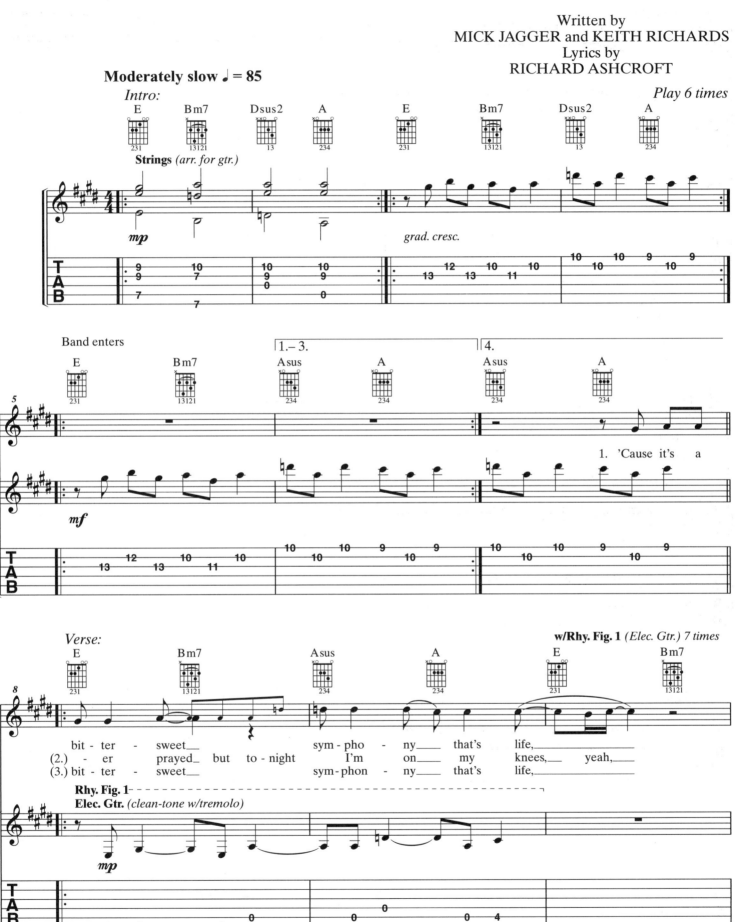

Bittersweet Symphony - 3 - 1

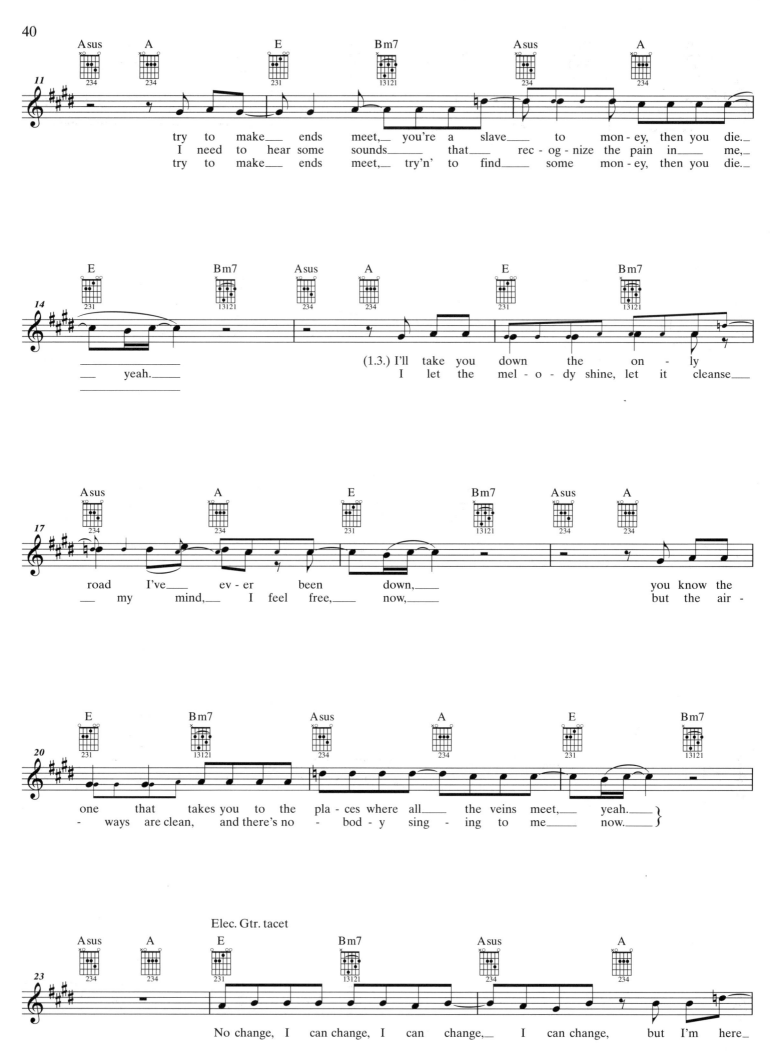

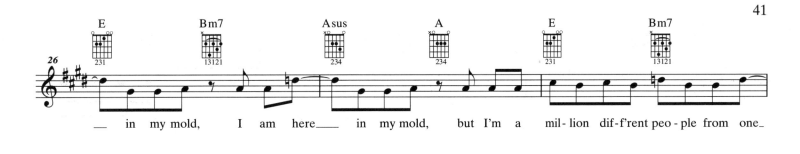

— in my mold, I am here___ in my mold, but I'm a mil - lion dif-f'rent peo - ple from one_

___ day to the next, I can't change my mold, no, no, no,___ no, no,___ no, no.___

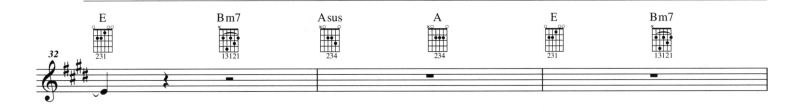

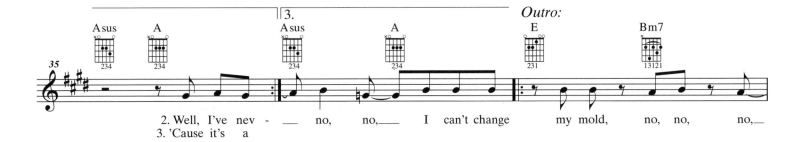

2. Well, I've nev - ___ no, no,___ I can't change my mold, no, no, no,___
3. 'Cause it's a

Repeat ad lib. and fade

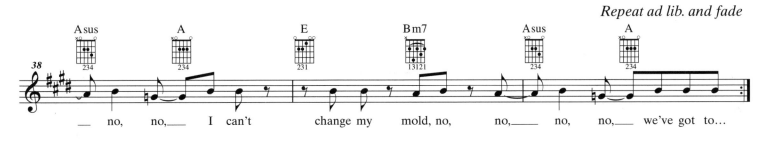

___ no, no,___ I can't change my mold, no, no,___ no, no,___ we've got to...

BECAUSE OF YOU

To match record key, Capo I

Words and Music by
KELLY CLARKSON, BEN MOODY
and DAVID HODGES

Slowly ♩ = 70

Intro:

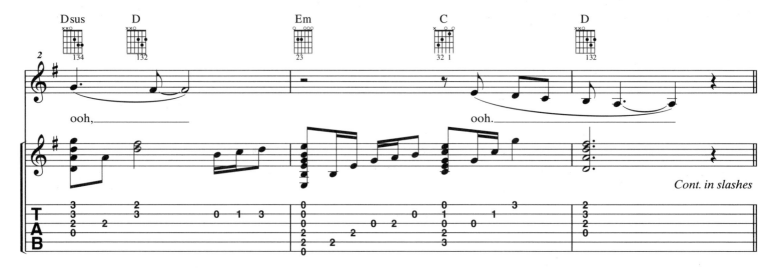

Verse:

Because of You - 4 - 1

G Bm Em(9) D
I will not break the way you did, you fell so hard.
I'm forced to fake a smile, a laugh ev - 'ry day of my
G Bm Em(9) Dsus D
I've learned the hard to nev - er let it get that far.
life. My heart can't pos - si - bly break when it was - n't e - ven whole to start with.
Be - cause of
Chorus:
Em C D Dsus D
you, I nev - er stray too far from the side - walk. Be - cause of
Em C D B7
Cont. rhy. simile
you, I learned to play on the safe side, so I don't get hurt. Be - cause of
Am7 G/B D B7
you, I find it hard to trust not on - ly me, but ev - 'ry - one a - round me. Be - cause of you,
Cmaj7 1. D 2. D
I am a - fraid. I watched you
Cont. in slashes

Bridge:

die, I heard you cry ev - 'ry night in your___ sleep. I was so
(I watched you die_____ in your

young, you should have known bet - ter than to lean___ on me._____ You nev - er
sleep.___ I was too young for you___ to lean on

thought of an - y - one else, you just saw your___ pain._____ And now I
me. You nev - er saw_____ me.__)

cry in the mid - dle of the night for the same damn thing._____ Be - cause of

Chorus:

you, I nev - er stray___ too far from the side - walk. Be - cause of

you, I learned to play on the safe side so I don't___ get hurt.__ Be - cause of

Because of You - 4 - 3

BILLIE JEAN

Words and Music by
MICHAEL JACKSON

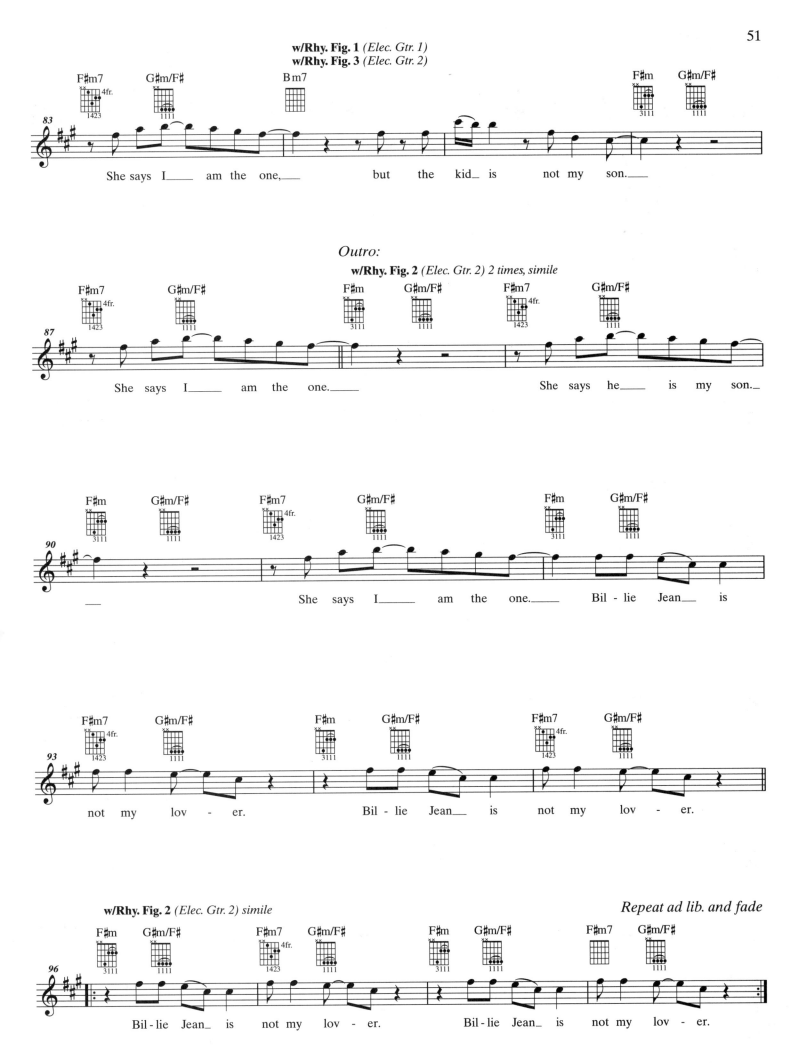

BLITZKRIEG BOP

Words and Music by
JEFFREY HYMAN, JOHN CUMMINGS,
DOUGLAS COLVIN and THOMAS ERDELYI

Blitzkrieg Bop - 2 - 1

BOULEVARD OF BROKEN DREAMS

Capo at 1st fret to match original recording.

Moderately fast ♩ = 86

Words by BILLIE JOE
Music by GREEN DAY

Boulevard of Broken Dreams - 3 - 1

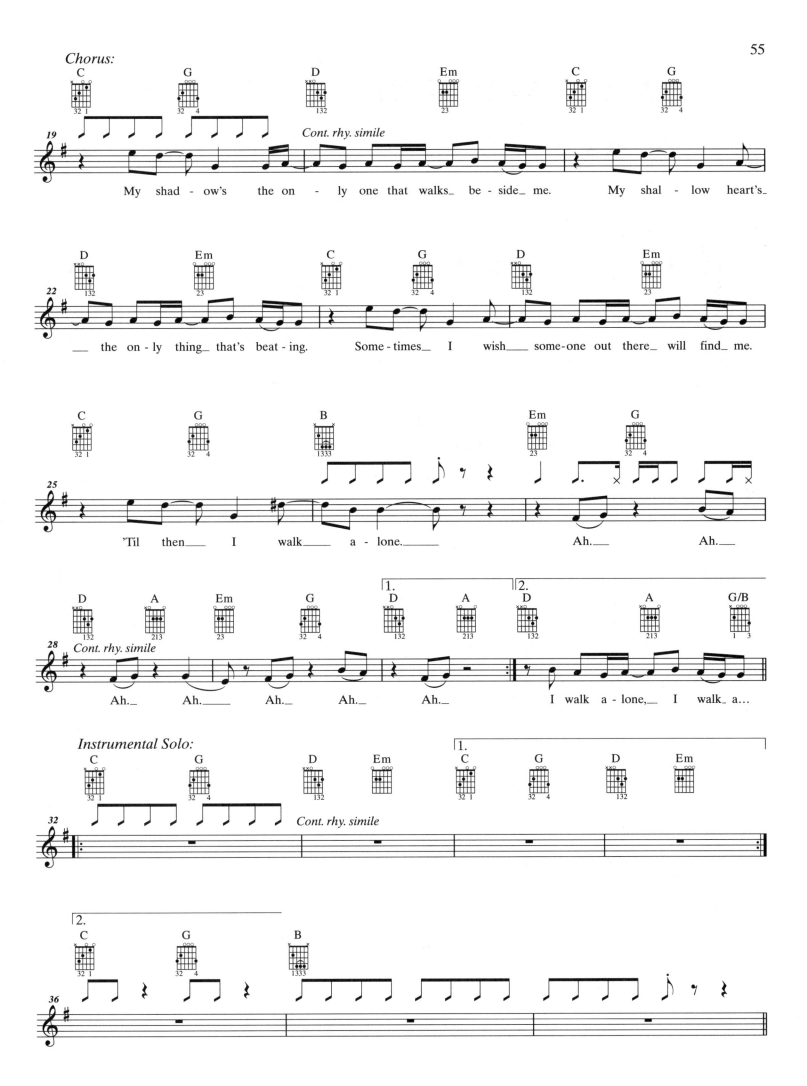

BROWN SUGAR

Words and Music by
MICK JAGGER and KEITH RICHARDS

Moderately ♩ = 126

Intro:

*Elec. Gtrs. 1 & 2 are both in open G tuning: ⑥ = D; ⑤ = G; ④ = D; ③ = G; ② = B; ① = D

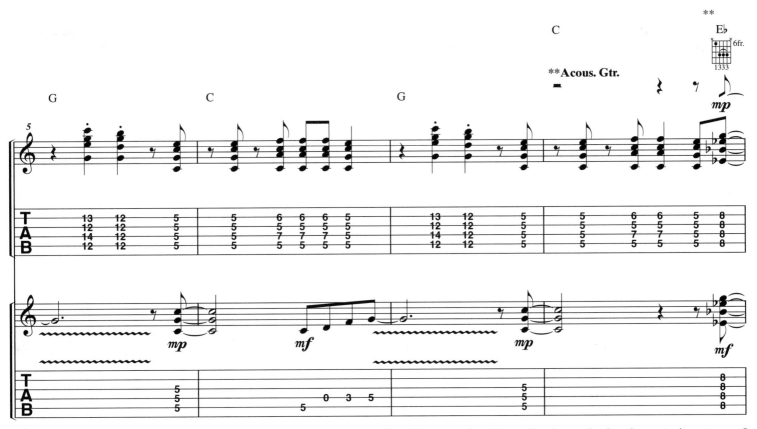

**Acous. Gtr.

**Chord frames reflect Acous. Gtr. in standard tuning, entering at meas. 8.

Brown Sugar - 7 - 1

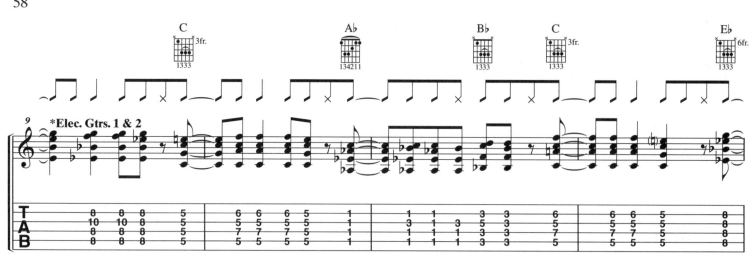

*Composite arrangement.

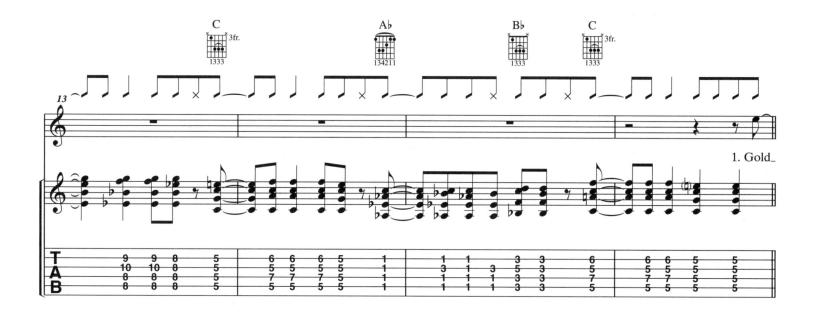

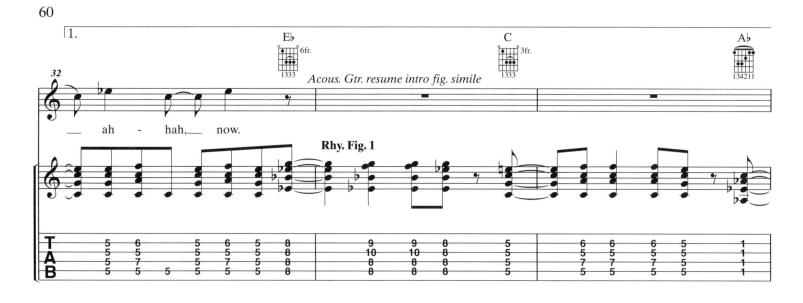

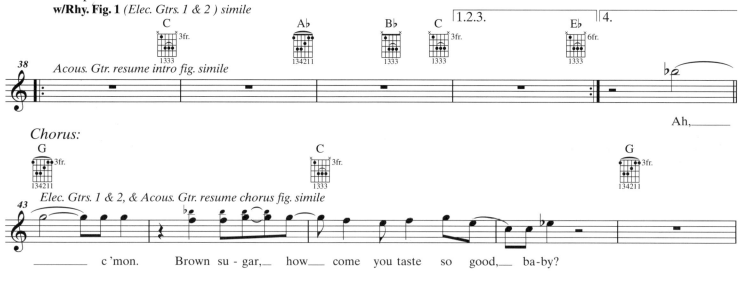

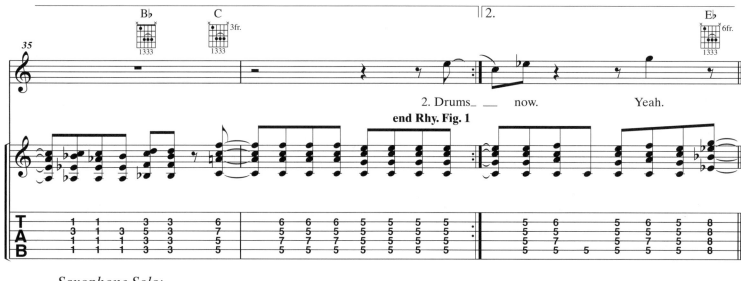

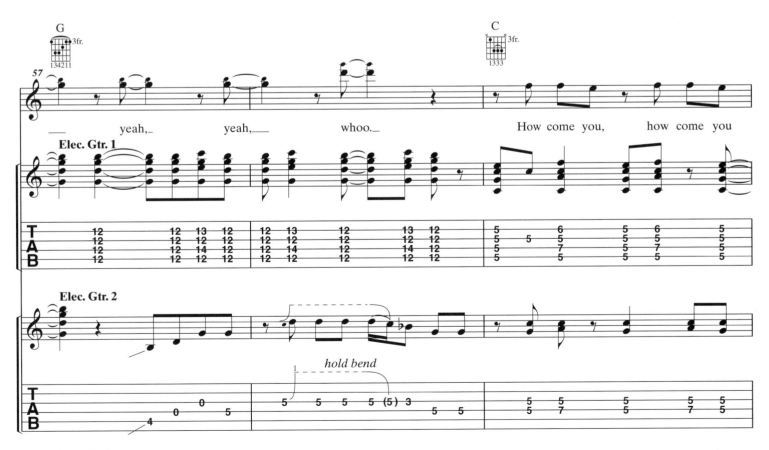

Verse 2:
Drums beating, cold English blood runs hot,
Lady of the house wondrin' where it's gonna stop.
House boy knows that he's doin' alright,
You should a heard him just around midnight.
(To Chorus:)

Verse 3:
I bet your mama was a tent show queen,
And all her boyfriends were sweet sixteen.
I'm no schoolboy but I know what I like,
You should have heard me just around midnight.
(To Chorus:)

BRAIN STEW

Lyrics by BILLIE JOE
Music by GREEN DAY

To match recorded key, tune down 1/2 step:

Moderately slow ♩ = 76

Verse 2:
My eyes feel like they're gonna bleed,
Dried up and bulging out my skull.
My mouth is dry,
My face is numb.
F***ed up and spun out in my room.
On my own.
Here we go.
(To Verse 3:)

Verse 3:
My mind is set on overdrive.
The clock is laughing in my face.
A crooked spine,
My sense is dulled.
Passed the point of delirium.
On my own.
Here we go.
(To Verse 4:)

Verse 4:
My eyes feel like they're gonna bleed,
Dried up and bulging out my skull.
My mouth is dry,
My face is numb.
F***ed up and spun out in my room.
On my own.
Here we go.
(To Outro:)

BRING ME TO LIFE

Moderately slow ♩ = 96

Words and Music by
BEN MOODY, AMY LEE and DAVID HODGES

Bring Me to Life - 4 - 1

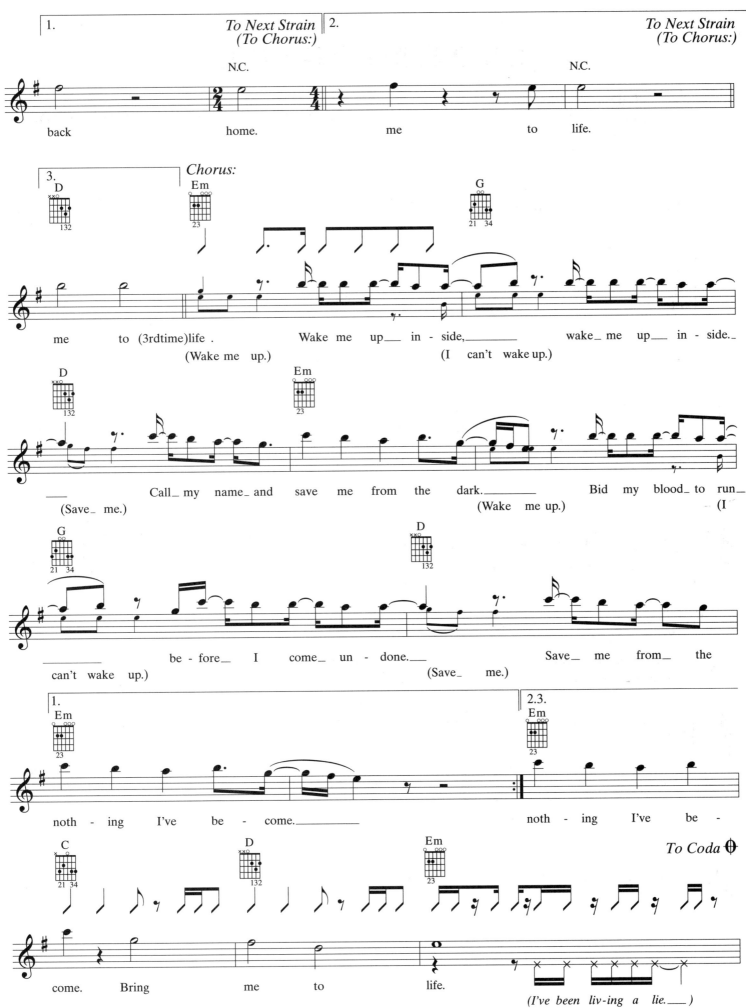

Verse 3:
All this time I can't believe I couldn't see.
Kept in the dark, but you were there in front of me.
I've been sleeping a thousand years, it seems.
Got to open my eyes to everything.
Without a thought, without a voice, without a soul,
Don't let me die here.
There must be something more.
Bring me to life.
(To Chorus:)

BROKEN
(Featuring Amy Lee)

Words and Music by
SHAUN WELGEMOED
and DALE STEWART

Slowly ♩ = 62

Intro:

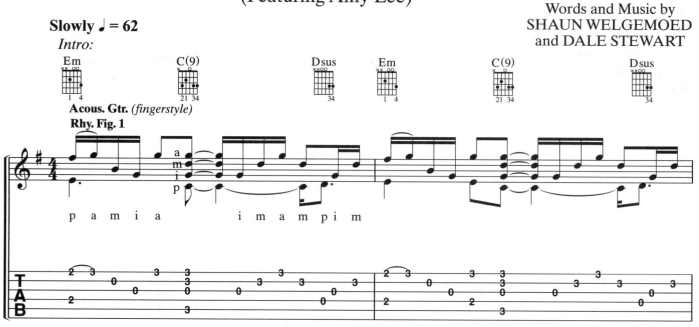

Verse:

1. I want-ed you to know___ that I love the way you laugh.___
2. The worst is o - ver now___ and we can breathe a - gain.___

Broken - 6 - 1

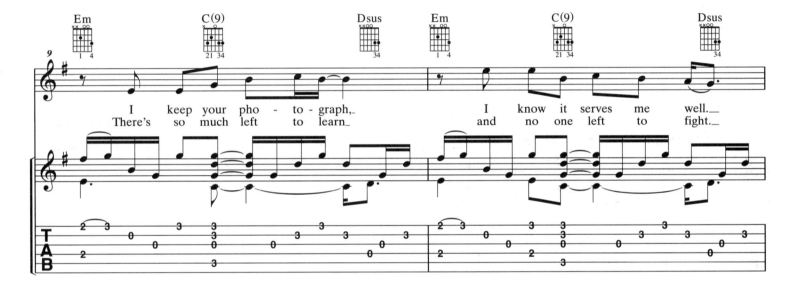

Cont. in slashes

Chorus:

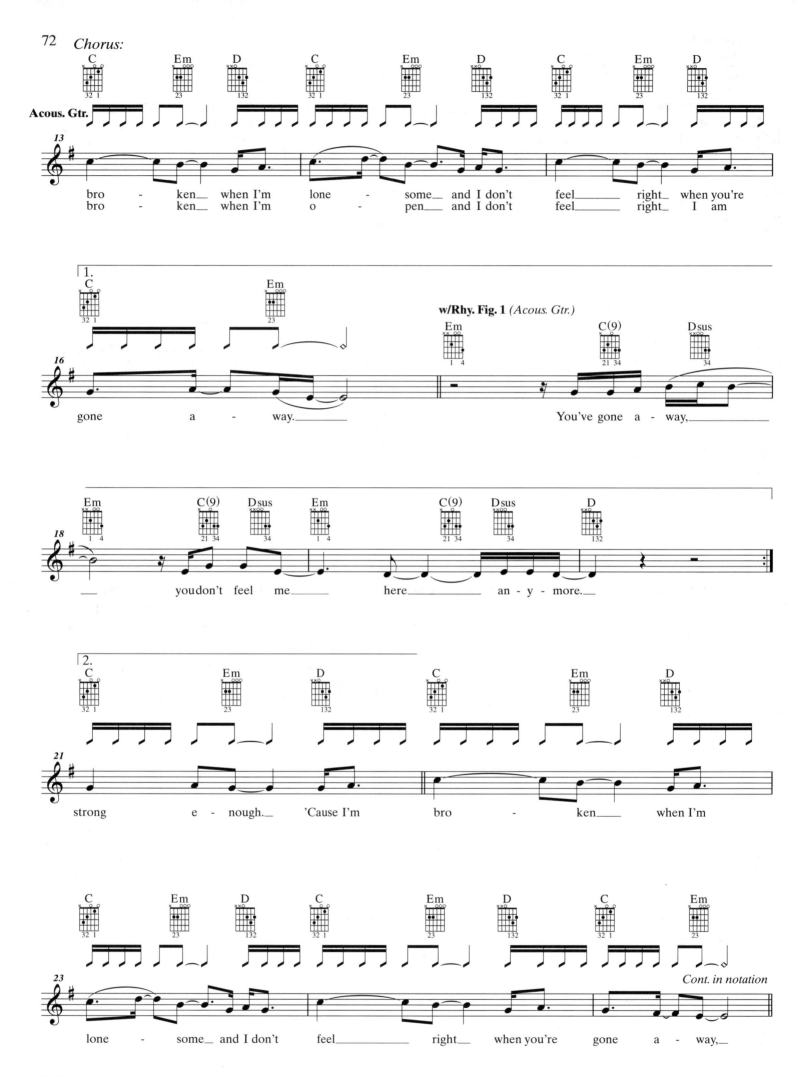

Guitar Solo:

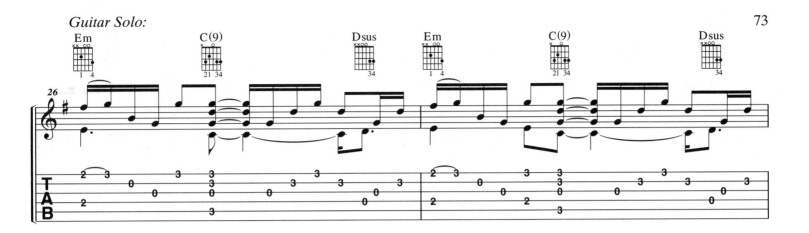

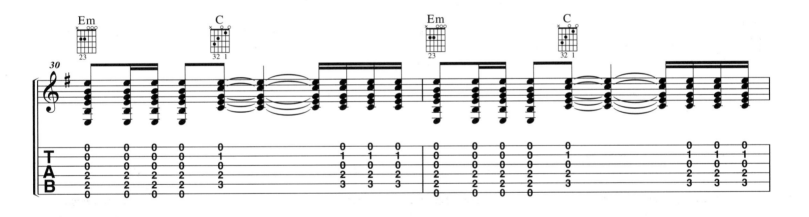

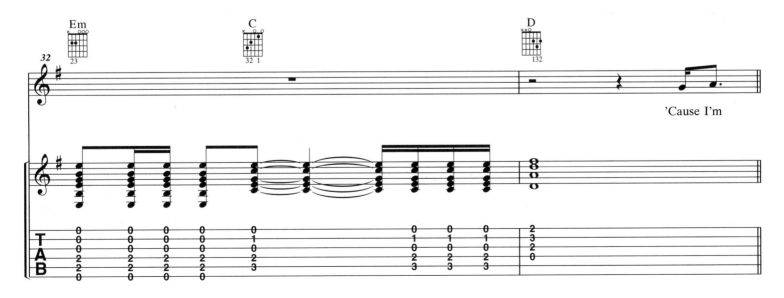

'Cause I'm

Chorus:

bro - ken___ when I'm o - pen___ and I don't

feel_____ right___ that I'm strong e nough.___ 'Cause I'm

Chorus:

bro_____ ken___ when I'm lone - some___ and I don't

feel_____ right___ when you're gone a - way.___

Elec. Gtr. *(w/dist.)*

'Cause I'm

Chorus:

bro - ken___ when I'm lone - some___ and I don't

feel_____ right___ when you're gone a - way._____

Outro:

You're gone a - way,_____ you don't feel me_____

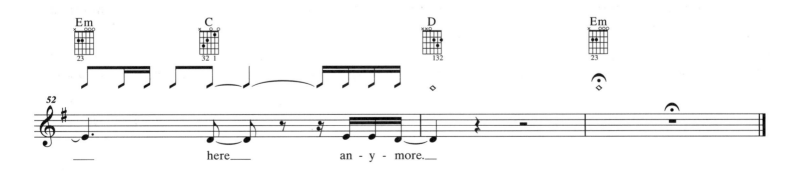

here___ an - y - more.___

A CHANGE WOULD DO YOU GOOD

Words and Music by
SHERYL CROW, BRIAN MacLEOD
and JEFF TROTT

To match record key, Capo I

Moderately fast ♩ = 130

1. Ten years liv-ing in a pa-per bag.___ Feed-back ba-by, he's a flipped out cat.___ He's a
2.3. *See additional lyrics*

plat-i-num ca-nar-y, drink in' Fal-staff beer.___ Mer-ce-des rule, and a rent-ed Lear.___

Pre-chorus:

1. Bot-tom feed-er in-sin-cere.___ Pro-phet lo-fi pi-o-neer.___
2.3. *See additional lyrics*

A Change Would Do You Good - 4 - 1

*Elec. Gtr. w/capo I (TAB numbers relative to capo).

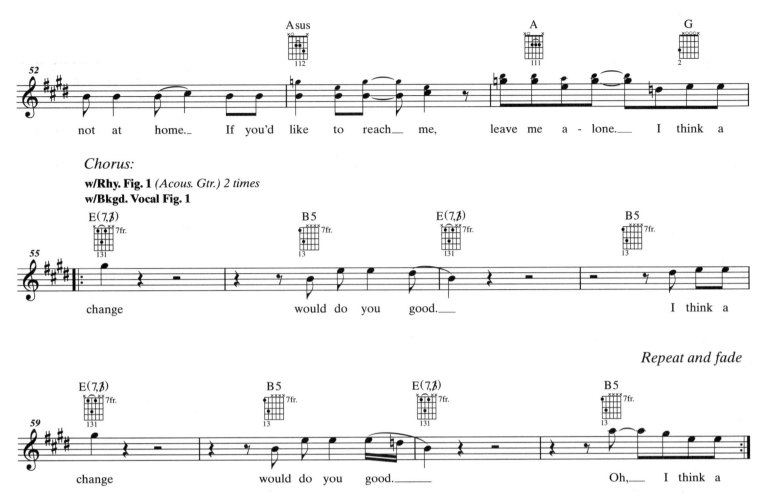

Chorus:

w/Rhy. Fig. 1 *(Acous. Gtr.) 2 times*
w/Bkgd. Vocal Fig. 1

Repeat and fade

Verse 2:
God's little gift is on the rag.
Poster girl posing in a fashion mag.
Canine, feline, Jekyll and Hyde?
Wear your fake fur on the inside.

Pre-chorus 2:
Queen of South Beach, aging blues.
Dinner's at six, wear your cement shoes.
I thought you were singing your heart out to me.
Your lips were syncing and now I see.
(To Chorus:)

Verse 3:
Chasing dragons with plastic swords.
Jack off Jimmy, everybody wants more.
Scully and Angel on the kitchen floor
And I'm calling Buddy on the Ouija board.

Pre-chorus 2:
I've been thinking íbout catching a train,
Leave my phone machine by the radar range.
Hello, it's me, I'm not at home.
If you'd like to reach me, leave me alone.
(To Chorus:)

COMPLICATED

Words and Music by
LAUREN CHRISTY, GRAHAM EDWARDS,
SCOTT SPOCK and AVRIL LAVIGNE

To match recorded key, tune down 1 whole step

Moderately ♩ = 78

Intro:

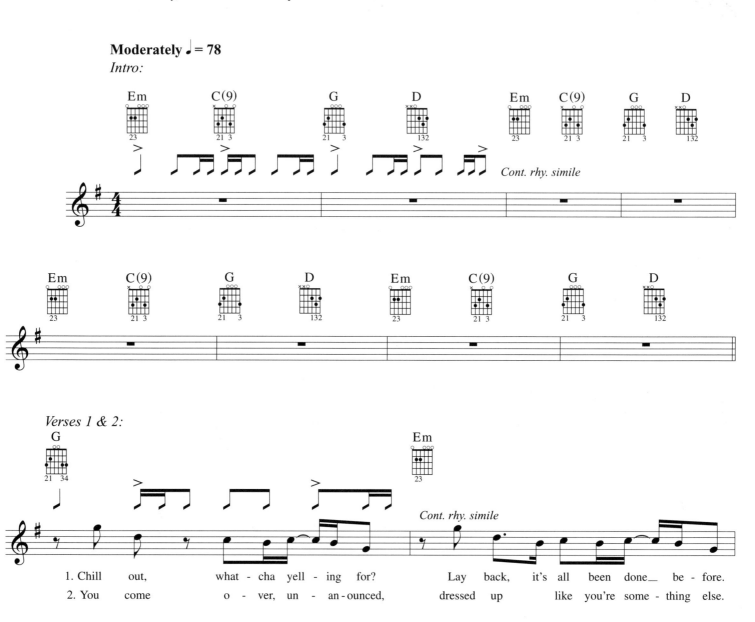

Verses 1 & 2:

1. Chill out, what-cha yell-ing for? Lay back, it's all been done__ be-fore.
2. You come o - ver, un - an-ounced, dressed up like you're some - thing else.

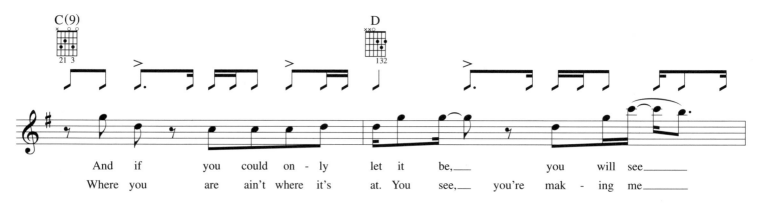

And if you could on - ly let it be,__ you will see_____
Where you are ain't where it's at. You see,__ you're mak - ing me

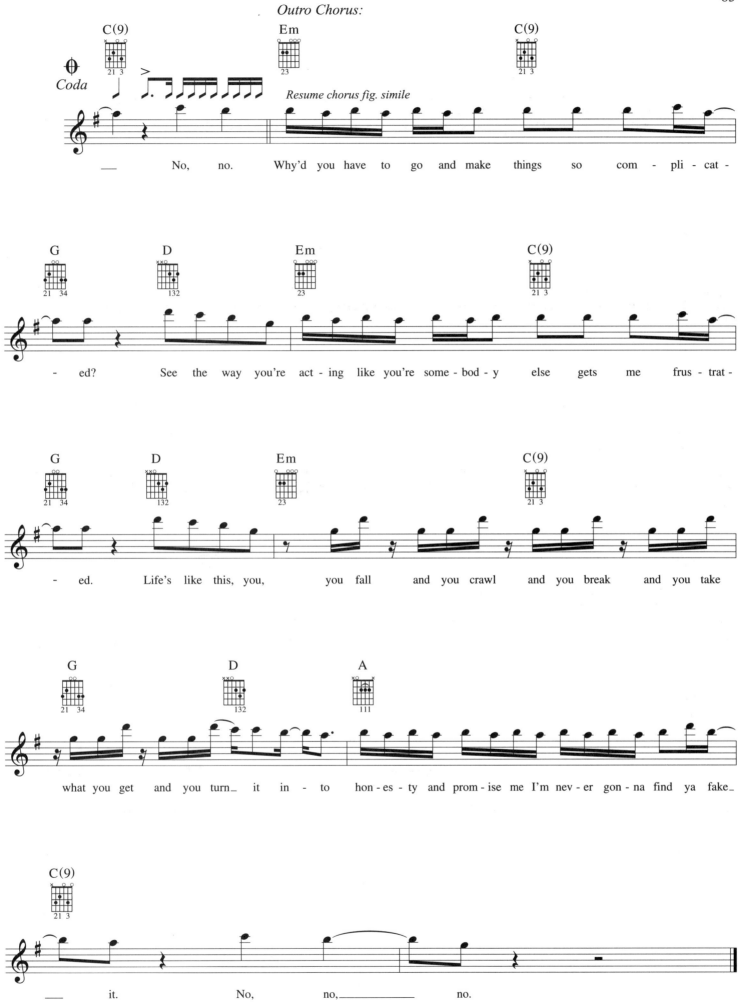

CRAZY

Words and Music by
THOMAS DECARLO CALLAWAY,
BRIAN JOSEPH BURTON,
GIANFRANCO REVERBERI
and GIAN PIERO REVERBERI

Moderately ♩ = 112

Crazy - 5 - 1

Crazy - 5 - 2

Crazy - 5 - 4

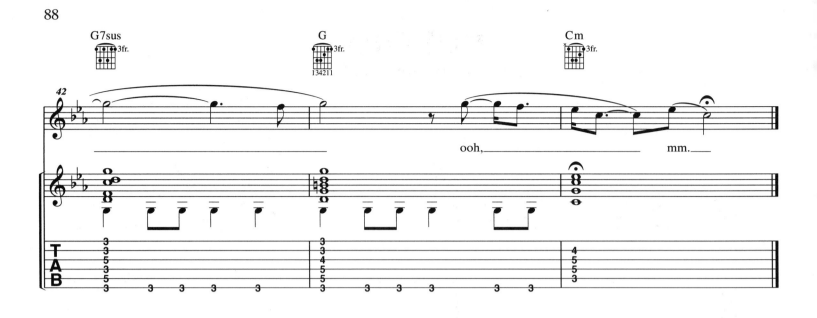

ooh,_____ mm.____

Verse 2:
Come on now, who do you, who do you,
Who do you, who do you think you are?
Ha ha ha, bless your soul,
You really think you're in control.

Chorus 2:
Well, I think you're crazy.
I think you're crazy.
I think you're crazy,
Just like me.
My heroes had the heart to lose their lives out on a limb,
And all I remember is thinking I want to be like them.

Verse 3:
Ever since I was little, ever since I was little, it looked like fun.
And it's no coincidence I've come,
And I can die when I'm done.

Chorus 3:
But maybe I'm crazy.
Maybe you're crazy.
Maybe we're crazy.
Probably.
(To Coda)

EUROPA
(Earth's Cry Heaven's Smile)

Words and Music by
CARLOS SANTANA and TOM COSTER

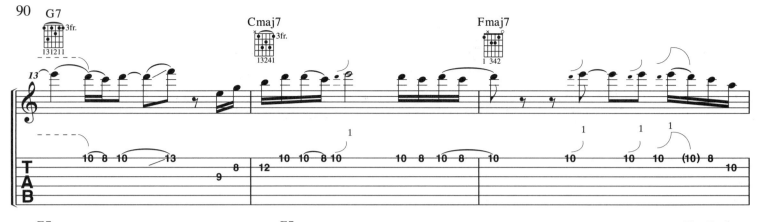

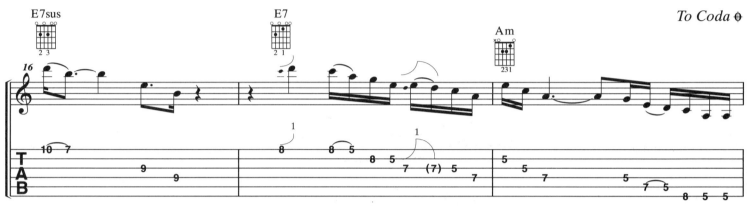

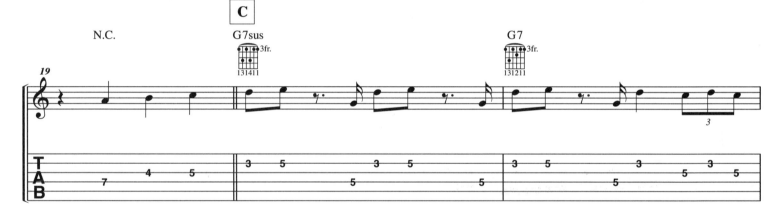

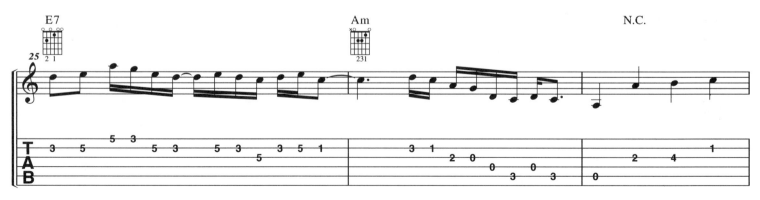

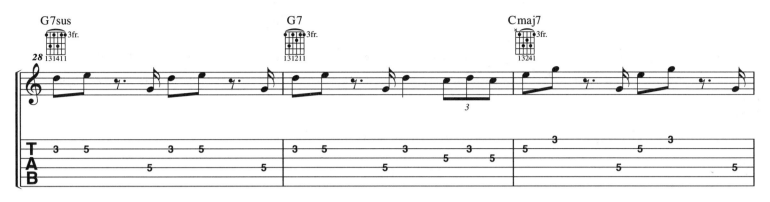

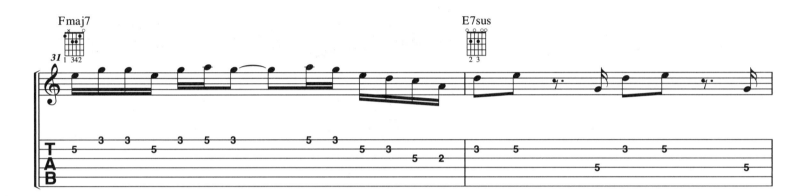

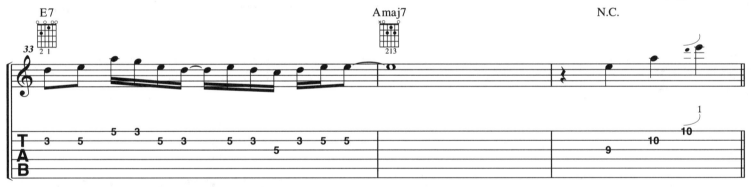

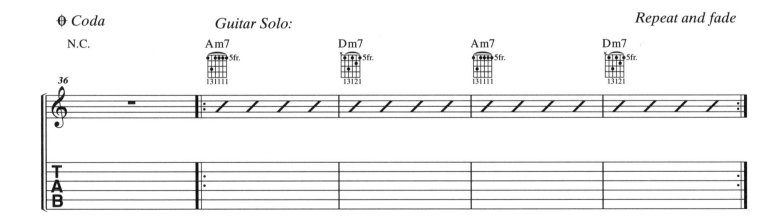

EVERYBODY'S FOOL

Tune to DADGAD:

⑥ = D ③ = G
⑤ = A ② = A
④ = D ① = D

Words and Music by
BEN MOODY, AMY LEE and DAVID HODGES

*Elec. Gtr. can also be played in Drop D

Moderately ♩ = 92

Intro:

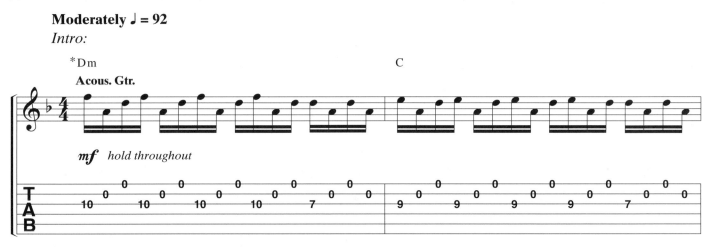

*Tune to DADGAD by tuning strings 6, 2, and 1 down a whole step.
As a result, strings 6 & 1 wil be octaves of string 4 and string 2 will be an octave of string 5.

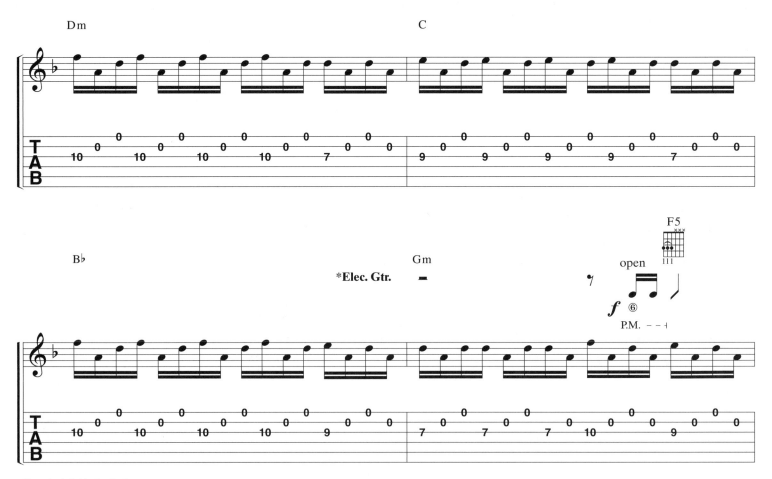

Everybody's Fool - 6 - 1

94

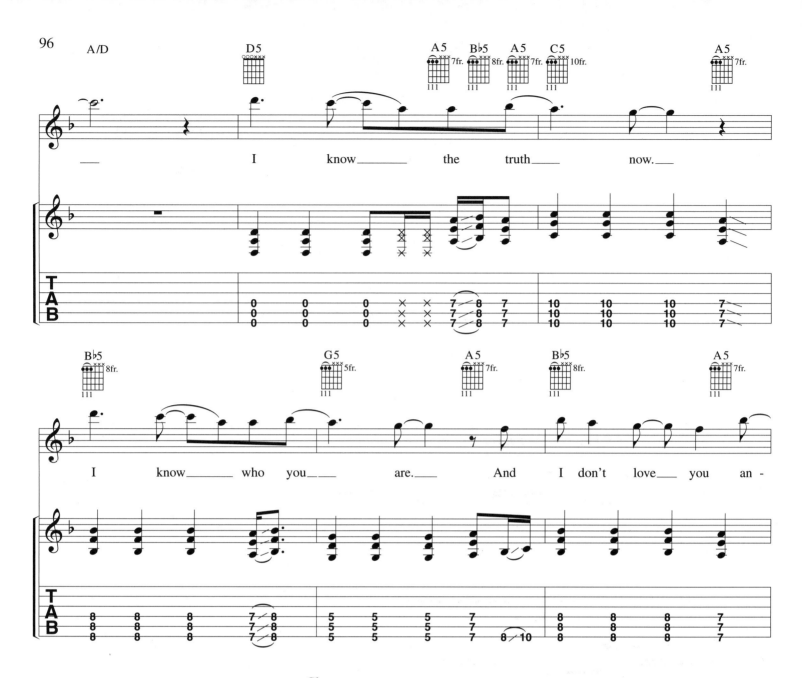

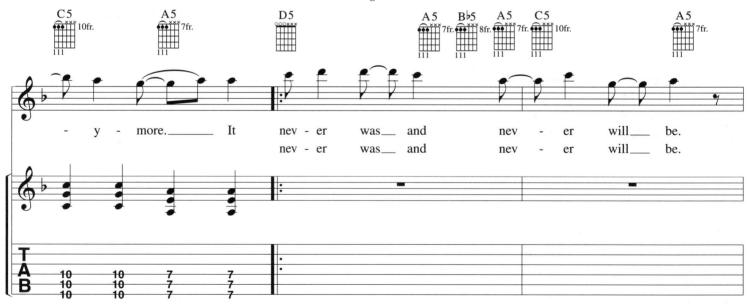

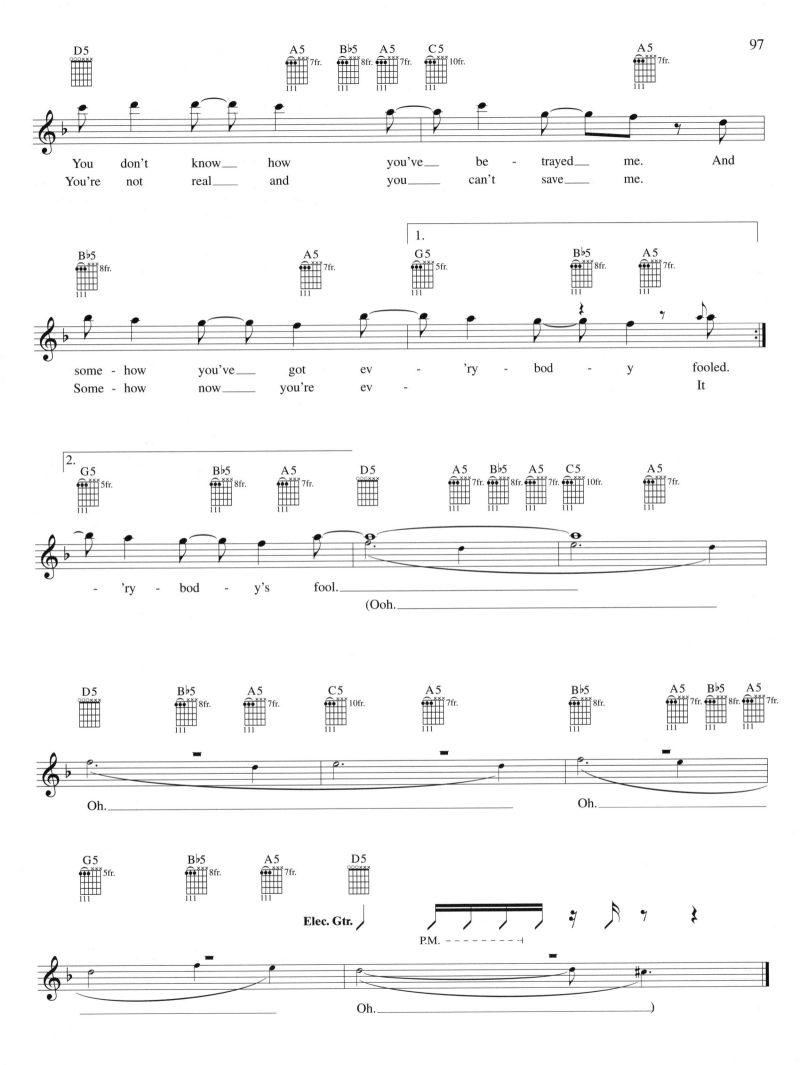

EVERYDAY PEOPLE

Words and Music by
SYLVESTER STEWART

Everyday People - 2 - 1

GOD SAVE THE QUEEN

Words and Music by
PAUL COOK, STEVE JONES,
GLEN MATLOCK and JOHNNY ROTTEN

Moderately fast ♩ = 140

Intro:

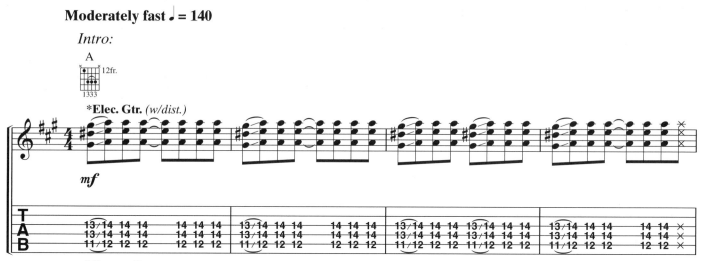

*Composite arrangement.

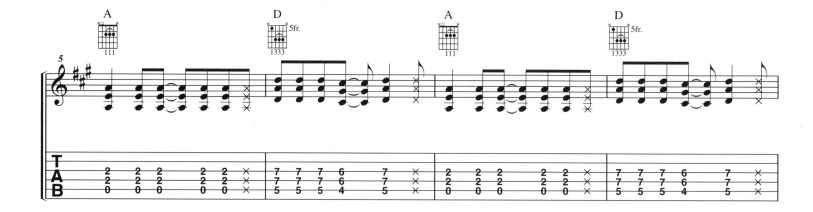

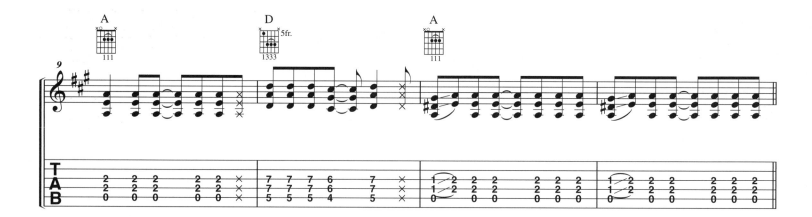

God Save the Queen - 6 - 1

Verse:

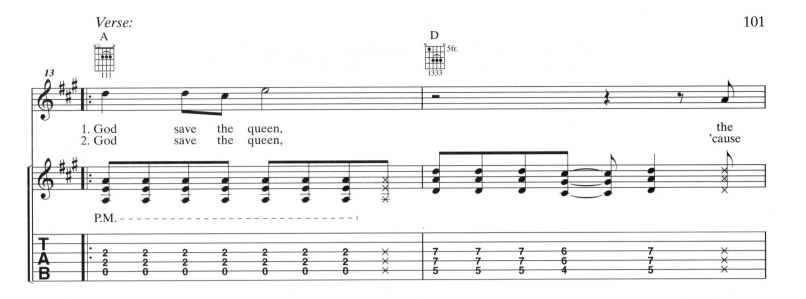

1. God save the queen,
2. God save the queen,

the 'cause

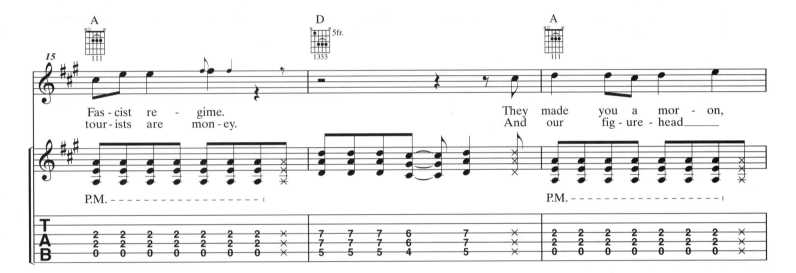

Fas - cist re - gime.
tour - ists are mon - ey.

They made you a mor - on,
And our fig - ure - head____

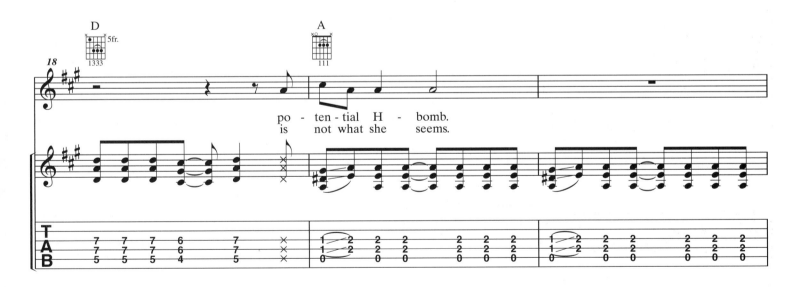

po - ten - tial H - bomb.
is not what she seems.

Elec. Gtr. cont. rhy. simile

God save the queen,
God save his - to - ry,

she ain't no hu - man be - ing.
God save your mad pa - rade.____

And
Oh,

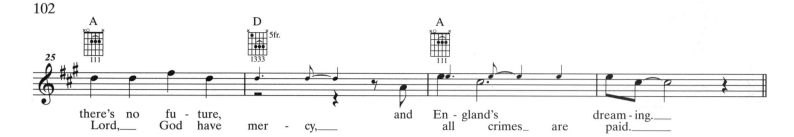

there's no fu - ture, and En - gland's dream - ing.___
Lord,___ God have mer - cy,___ all crimes_ are paid.___

Pre-chorus:

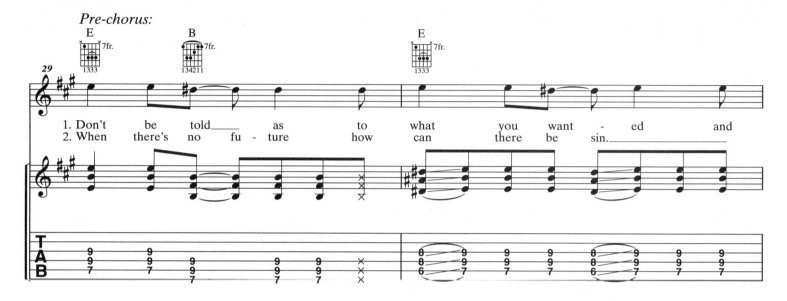

1. Don't be told___ as to what you want - ed and
2. When there's no fu - ture how what can there be sin.___

don't be told___ as to what you need._ There's no fu - ture,
We're the flow - ers in to the dust - bin.___ We're the poi - son in the

no fu - ture, no fu - ture for you.
hu - man ma-chine. We're the fu - ture, your fu - ture.}

Chorus:

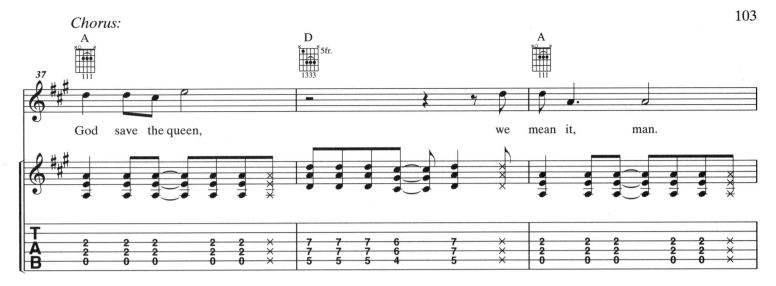

God save the queen, we mean it, man.

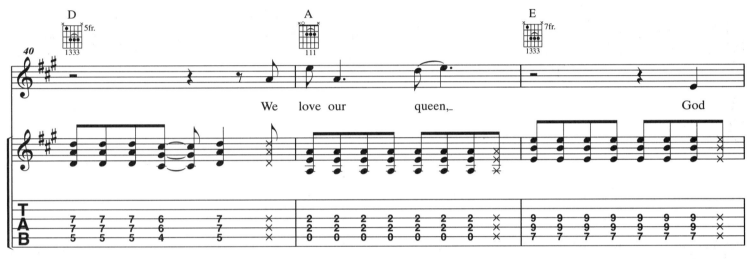

We love our queen,— God

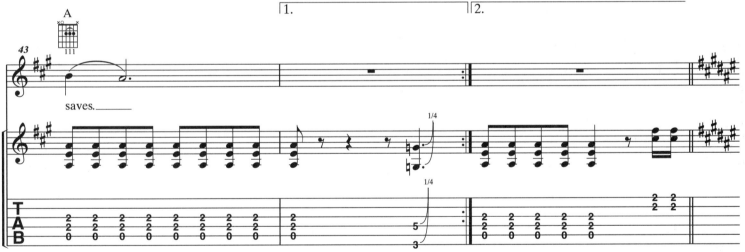

saves.——

Guitar Solo:

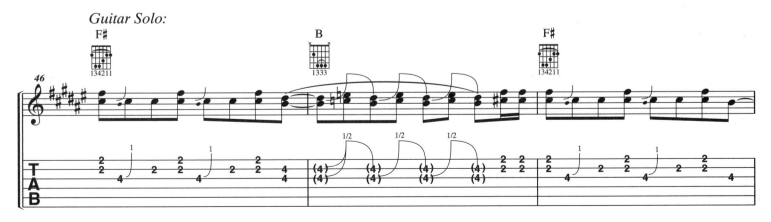

God Save the Queen - 6 - 4

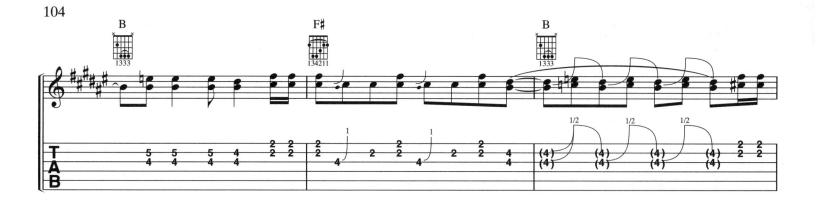

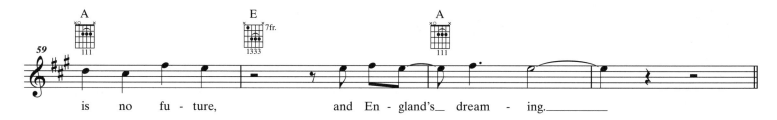

Chorus:

God save the queen, we mean it, man. There

is no fu - ture, and En - gland's__ dream - ing._____

Outro:

No fu - ture, no

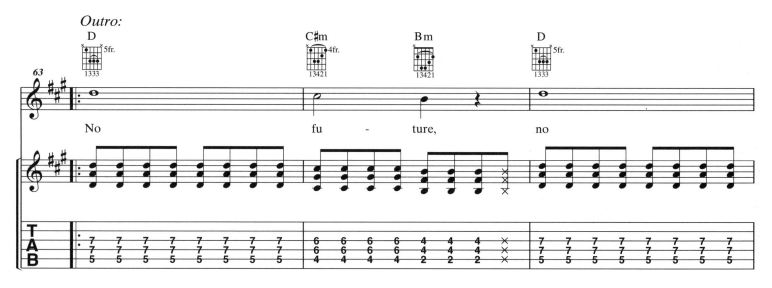

God Save the Queen - 6 - 5

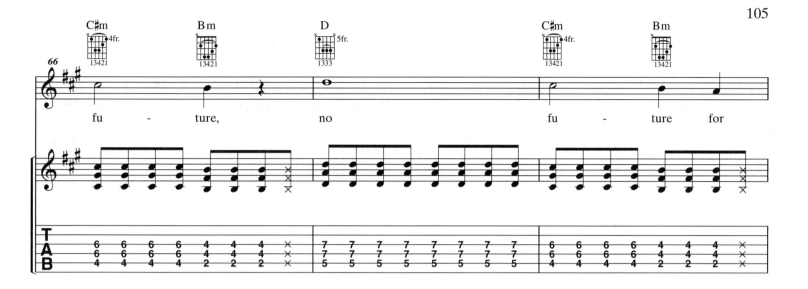

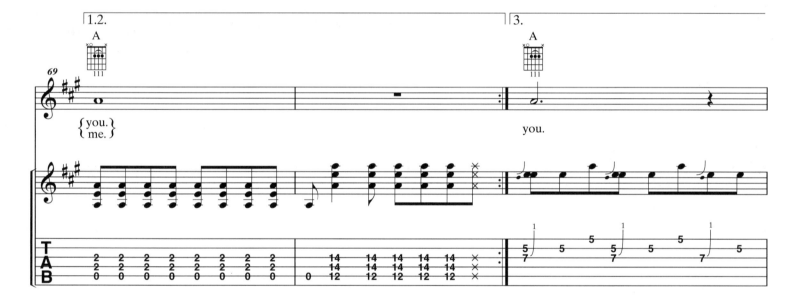

GOING UNDER

Words and Music by
BEN MOODY, AMY LEE and DAVID HODGES

Going Under - 3 - 1

tor - ment - ed dail - y,___ de - feat - ed___ by you.___ Just when
Al - ways___ con - fus - ing___ the thoughts in___ my head.___

I thought I'd reached___ the bot - tom.___
So I can't trust my - self___ an - y - more...___ }

G A Em

I'm___ dy - ing a - gain.___ I'm go - ing un -

B5 G5 D5 A/C#

- der___ drown - ing in you.
(Go - ing un - der.)

B5 G5 D5 A/C#

Cont. rhy. simile

I'm fall - ing for ev -
(Drown - ing in you.___)

B5 G5 D5 A/C#

- er,___ I've got to break___
(Fall - ing for ev - er.)

To Coda ⊕ | 1.

B5 G5 D5 A/C# B5

___ through.___ I'm___ go - ing un - der.___
Going Under - 3 - 2   (I'm___ go - ing....)

Going Under - 3 - 3

HIGHER

Gtr. tuned in Drop D:
⑥ = D   ③ = G
⑤ = A   ② = B
④ = D   ① = E

Words and Music by
MARK TREMONTI and SCOTT STAPP

Slow rock ♩ = 80

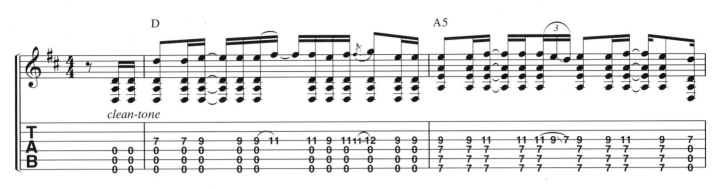

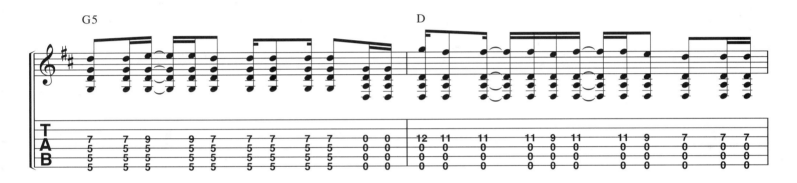

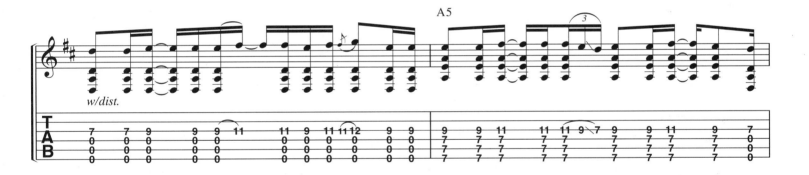

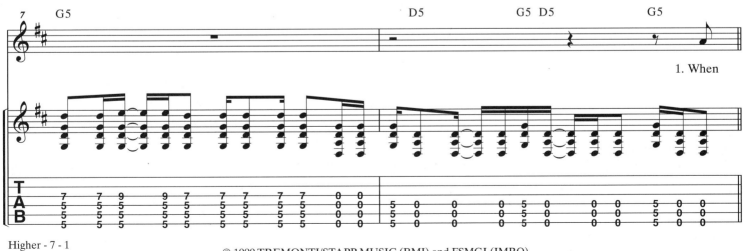

1. When

Higher - 7 - 1

Chorus:

dream - in',_____ I got in - to_ an - oth - er world_ time and time_ a -
though I_____ would like a world_ of change,_____ it helps me to___ a -

clean-tone

gain._____ At
pre - ci - ate those nights and those dreams._____ But,

sun - rise,_____ I fight to stay_ a - sleep_____ 'cause I don't wan - na leave the
my friend,_____ I'd sac - ri - fice_____ all those nights if I_____ could make_ the

Rhy. Fig. 1

Higher - 7 - 3

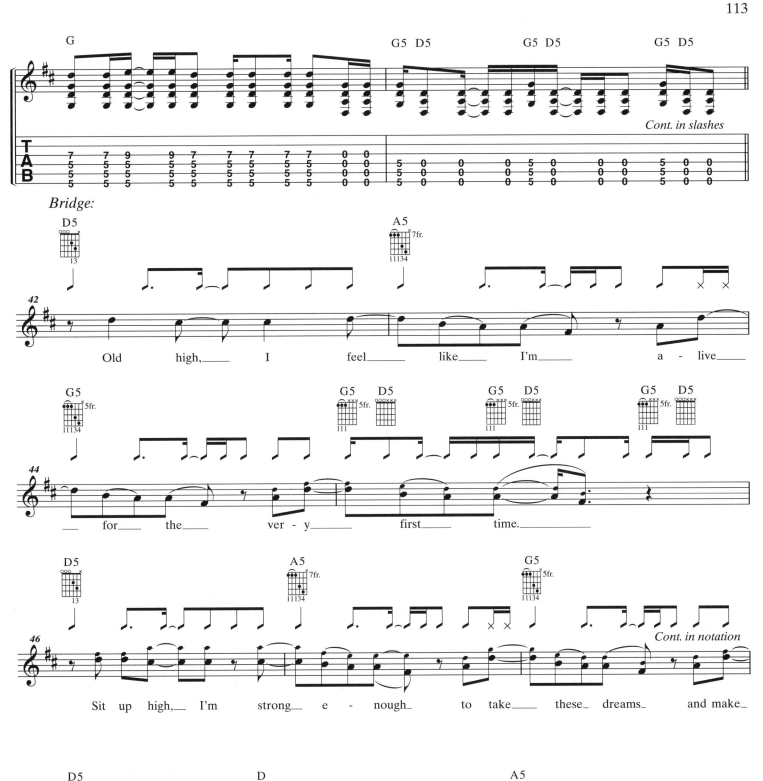

Bridge:

Old high,___ I feel___ like___ I'm___ a - live___ ___ for___ the___ ver - y___ first___ time.___

Sit up high,___ I'm strong___ e - nough___ to take___ these_ dreams_ and make_

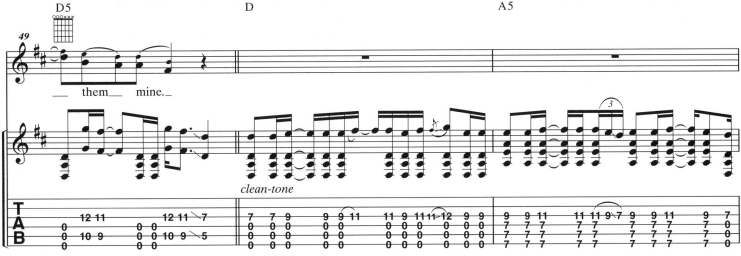

___ them_ mine._

clean-tone

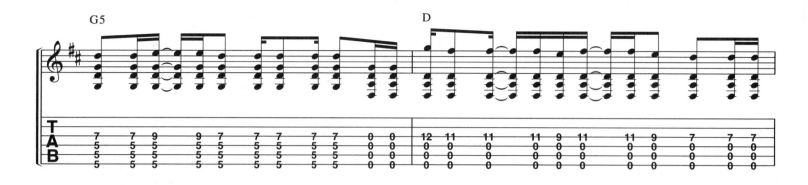

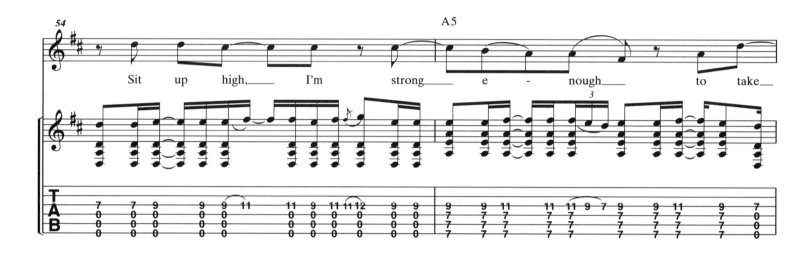

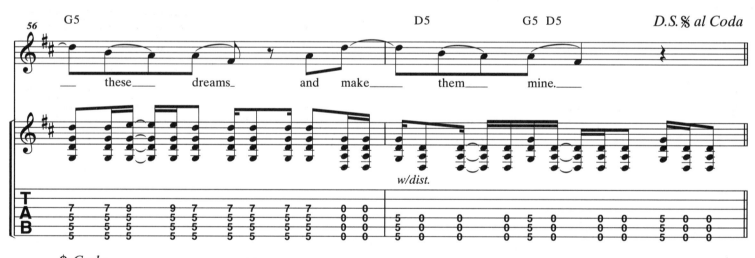

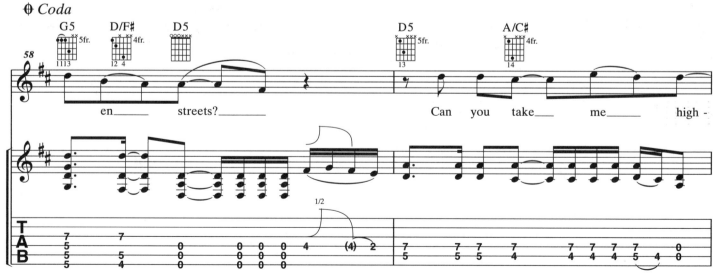

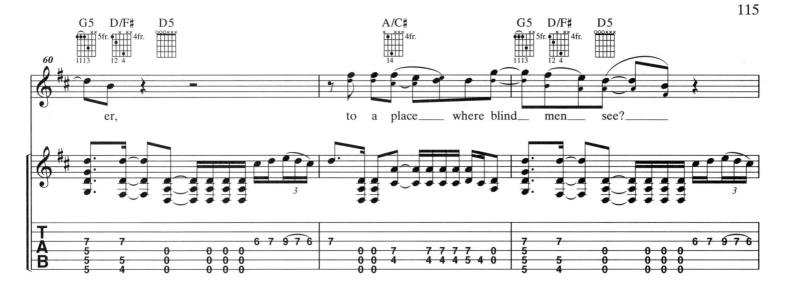

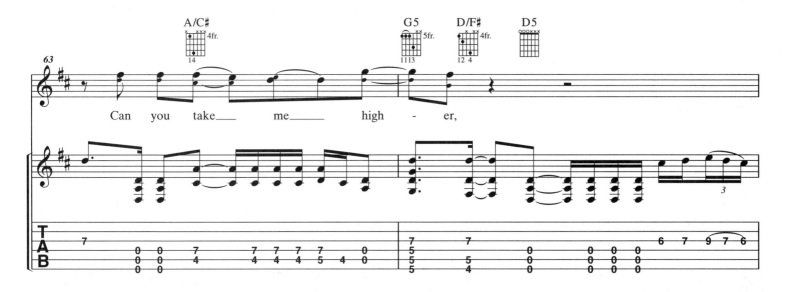

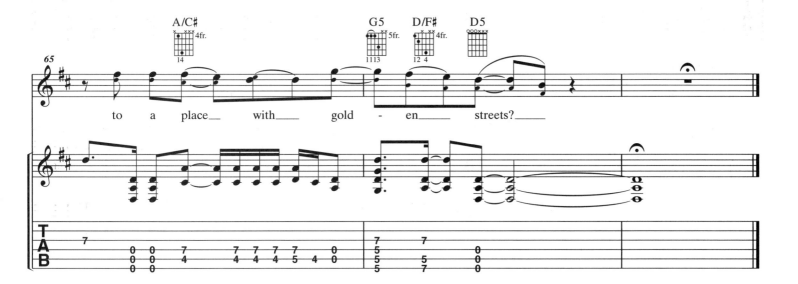

HEADSTRONG

Music by
CHRIS BROWN, PETER CHARELL
and SIMON ORMANDY
Lyrics by
CHRIS BROWN

Moderate rock ♩ = 92

Intro:

1. Cir - cl - ing, you're cir - cl - ing, you're

Verse:

cir - cl - ing your head, con - tem - plat - ing ev - 'ry thing you ev - er said. Now I see the
clu - sions man - i - fest your first im - pres - sion's got to be your ver - y best. I see you're full of

Headstrong - 4 - 1

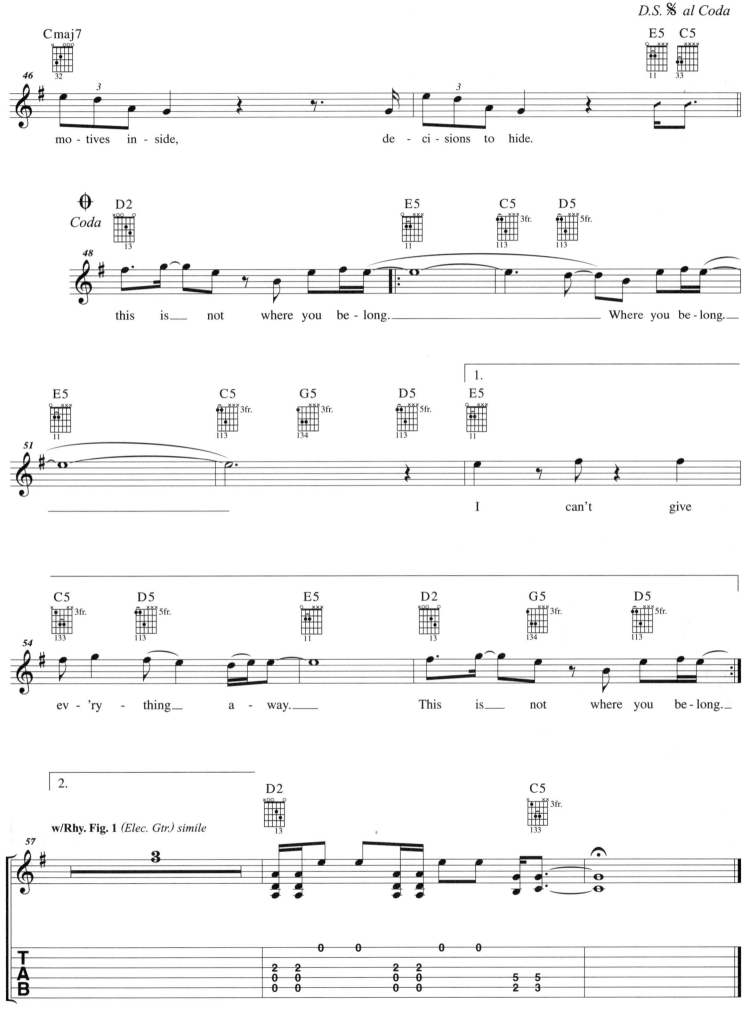

Headstrong - 4 - 4

HONKY TONK WOMEN

Words and Music by
MICK JAGGER and KEITH RICHARDS

Honky Tonk Women - 5 - 1

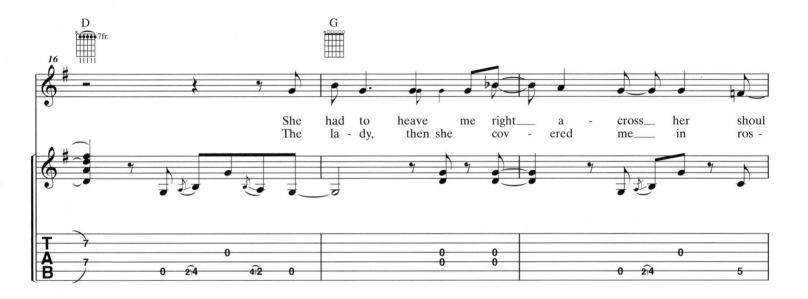

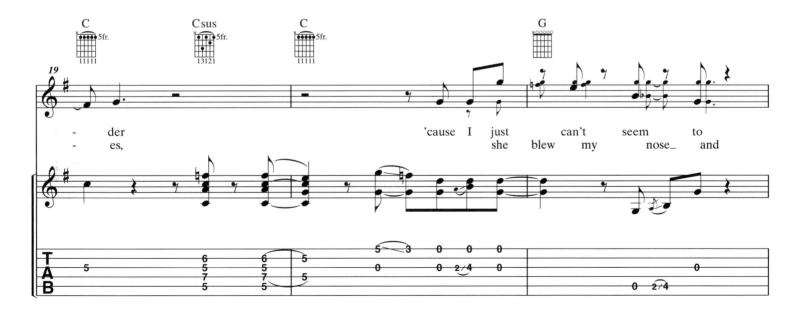

Honky Tonk Women - 5 - 2

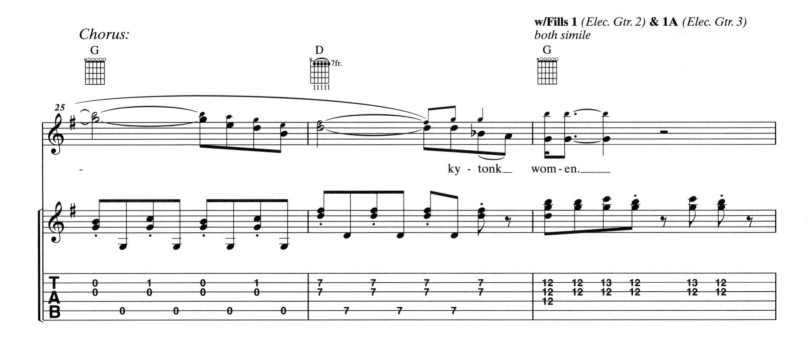

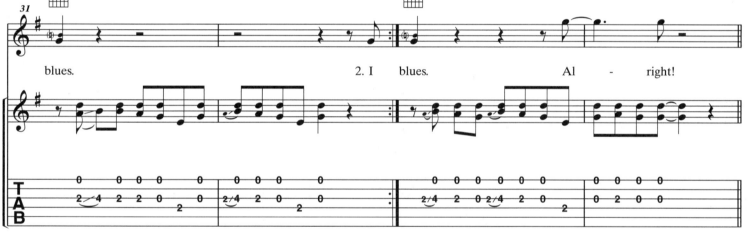

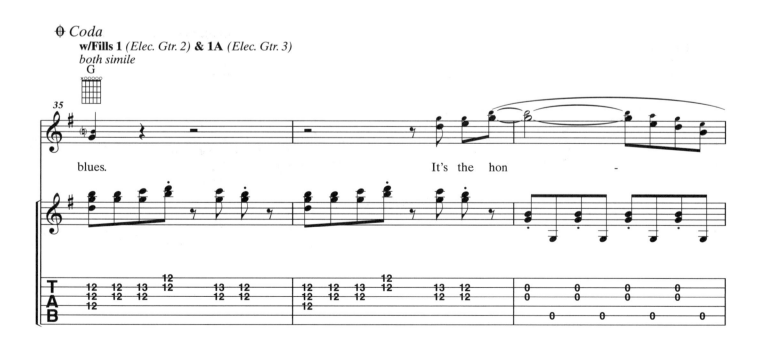

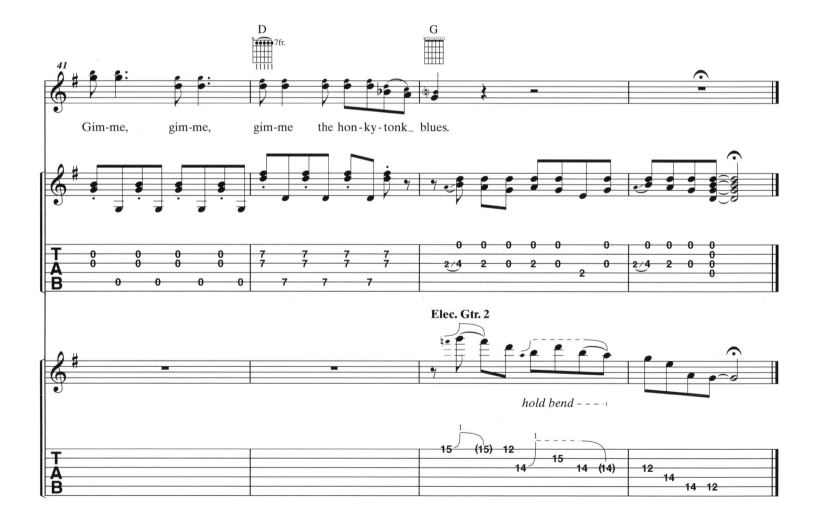

HOW YOU REMIND ME

Lyrics by
CHAD KROEGER
Music by
NICKELBACK

How You Remind Me - 3 - 1

Verse 2:
It's not like you didn't know that.
I said I love you and I swear I still do.
And it must have been so bad.
'Cause livin' with me must have damn near killed you.
(To Chorus:)

I DON'T WANT TO BE

Capo 1st fret to match recording

Words and Music by
GAVIN DeGRAW

I Don't Want to Be - 4 - 1

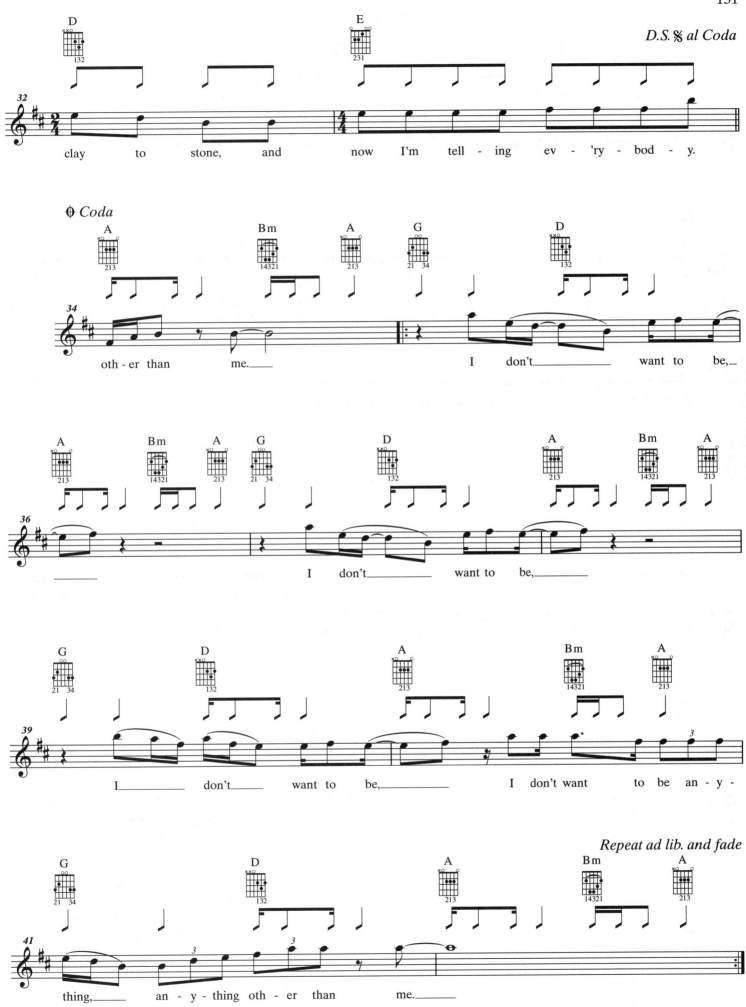

I'LL STAND BY YOU

(as recorded by the Pretenders)

Words and Music by
BILLY STEINBERG, TOM KELLY
and CHRISSIE HYNDE

I'll Stand by You - 4 - 1

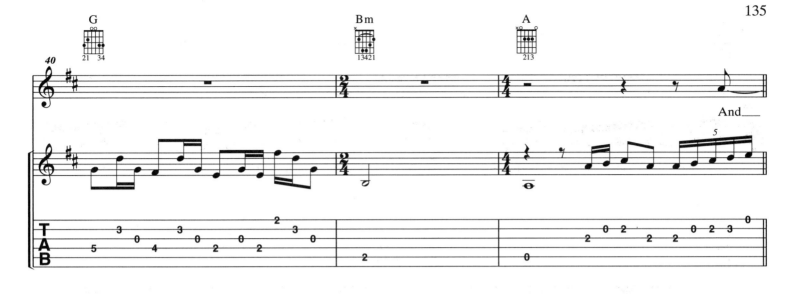

And___

___ when,___ when the night_ falls___ on you, baby,___ you're feel-ing all a-

D.S. % al Coda

lone,___ you won't be on___ your own. I'll stand_ by

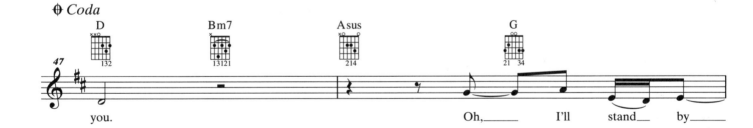

you. Oh,___ I'll stand__ by___

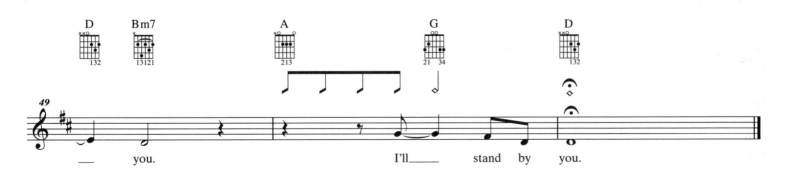

___ you. I'll___ stand by you.

IMMIGRANT SONG

Words and Music by
JIMMY PAGE and ROBERT PLANT

Moderately ♩ = 112

Intro:

simile throughout

Ah, _____ ah.

Verse:

A | E

1. I come from the land of the ice and snow, from the
come from the land of the ice and snow, from the

A | F#m

mid - night sun where the hot springs flow.___ Ham - mer of___ the gods will
mid - night sun where the hot springs flow.___ How soft your fields so green, can

Immigrant Song - 3 - 1

LISTEN TO THE MUSIC

Words and Music by
TOM JOHNSTON

Moderately ♩ = 104

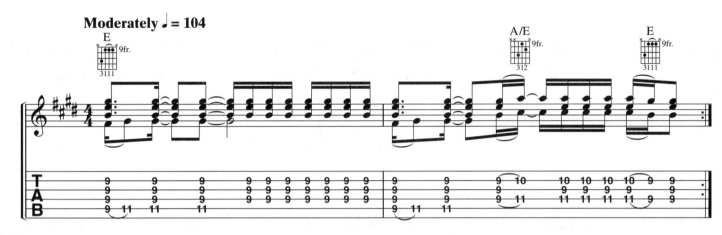

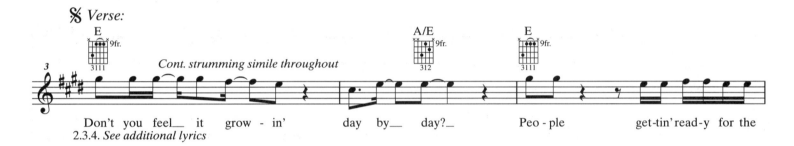

%% *Verse:*

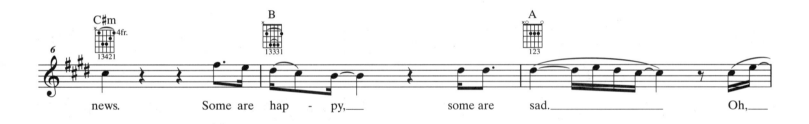

Don't you feel__ it grow - in' day by__ day?__ Peo - ple get-tin' read-y for the
2.3.4. *See additional lyrics*

news. Some are hap - py,__ some are sad._____ Oh,__

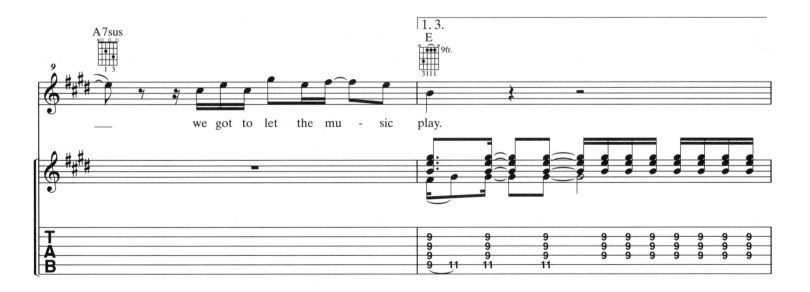

__ we got to let the mu - sic play.

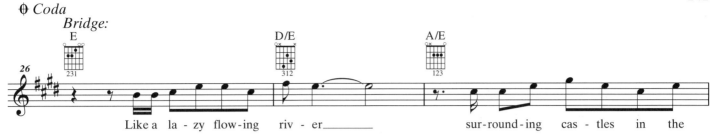

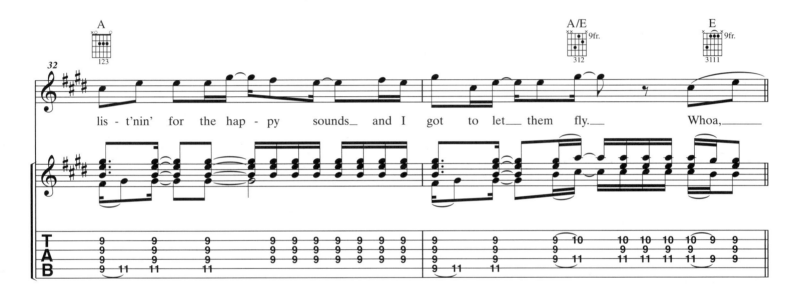

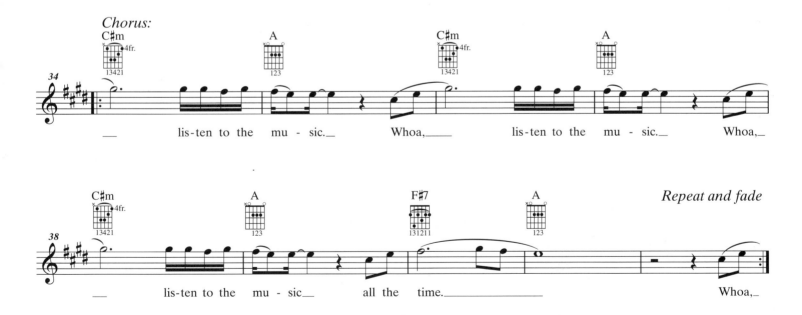

MINORITY

Moderately ♩ = 132 (♫ = ♩♪ triplet)

Lyrics by BILLIE JOE
Music by GREEN DAY

Intro:

C G Fmaj7 C G F C
Chorus:
C5 F5 G5 F5 C5 F5 G5 F5
3fr.
I want to be the mi - nor - i - ty. I don't need your au - thor - i - ty.
Down with the mor - al ma - jor - i - ty. 'Cause I want to be the mi - nor - i - ty. 1. I
Verse:
C G Fmaj7 C G
pledge al - le - giance to the un - der - world. One na - tion un - der - dog there of
(2.3.) light, one mind flash - ing in the dark. Blind - ed by the si - lence of a
F G C G Fmaj7 C
which I stand a - lone. A face in the crowd, un - sung a - gainst the mold. With -
thou - sand bro - ken hearts. "For cry - ing out loud," she screamed un - to me. A

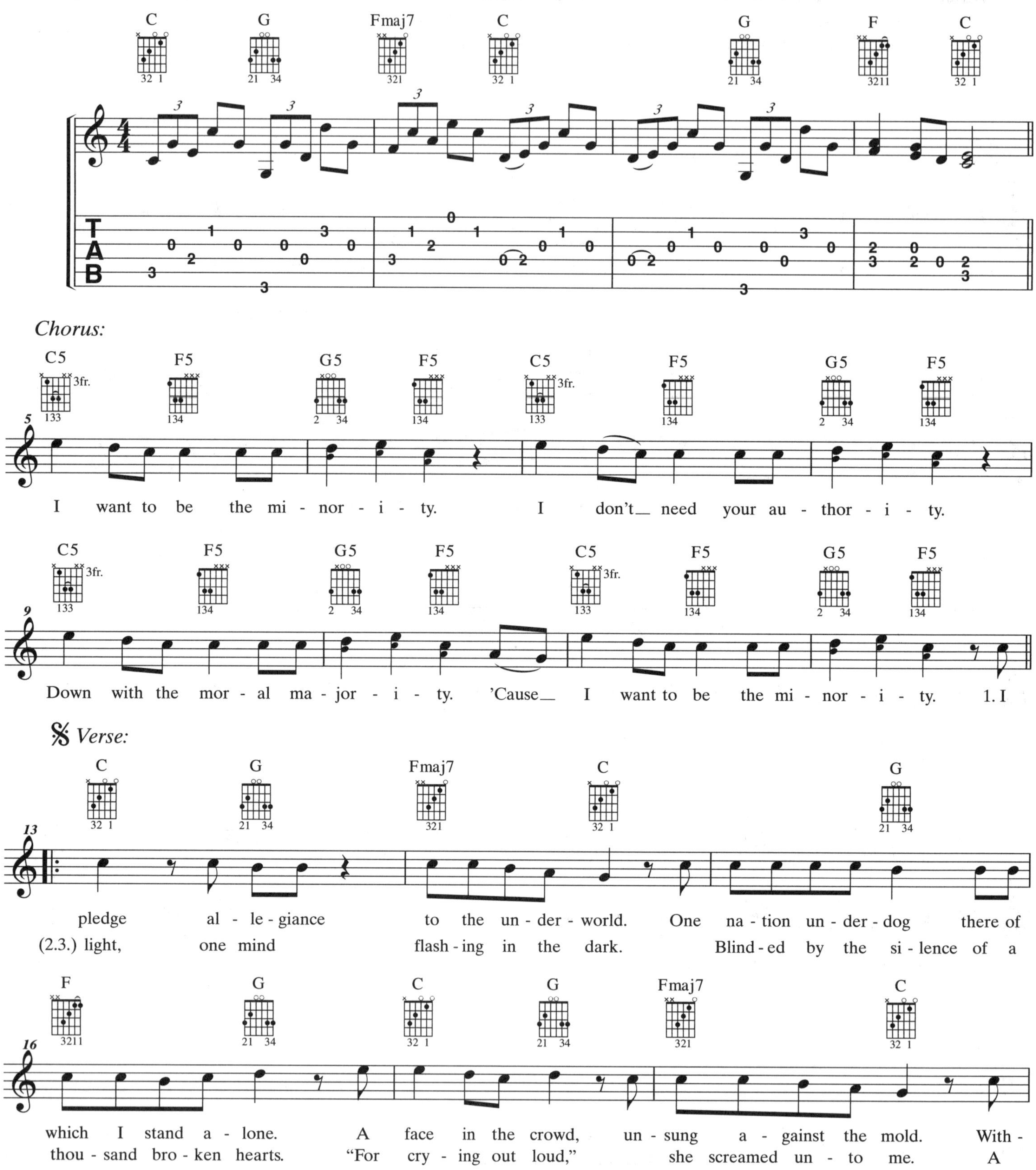

144

Outro:

MY IMMORTAL

Words and Music by
BEN MOODY, AMY LEE and DAVID HODGES

To match recording, capo at 2nd fret.

Slowly and freely ♩ = 80

My Immortal - 3 - 1

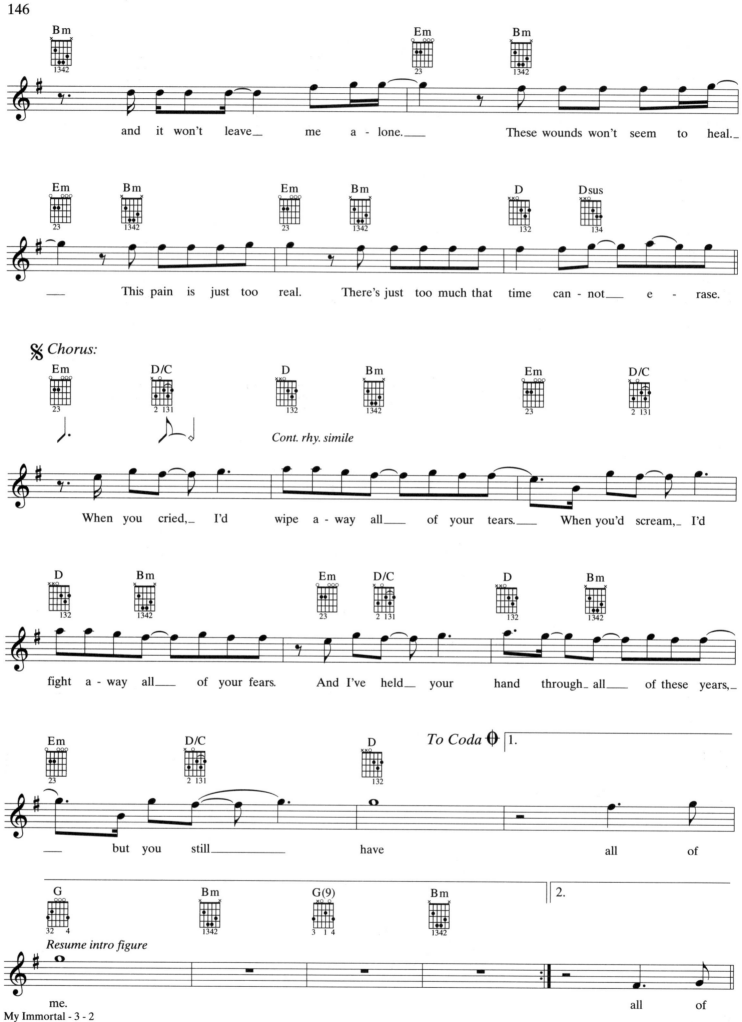

all, me.

Verse 2:
You used to captivate me
By your resonating light.
But, now I'm bound by the life you left behind.
Your face, it haunts
My once pleasant dreams.
Your voice, it chased away
All the sanity in me.
These wounds won't seem to heal.
This pain is just too real.
There's just too much that time can not erase.
(To Chorus:)

MISERY BUSINESS

To match record key, tune down one half step.

Words and Music by
HAYLEY WILLIAMS and JOSH FARRO

Verse:

1. I'm in the bus-'ness of mis - er - y, let's take it from the
2. Sec - ond chanc - es, they don't nev - er mat - ter, peo - ple nev - er

Misery Business - 8 - 1

Chorus:

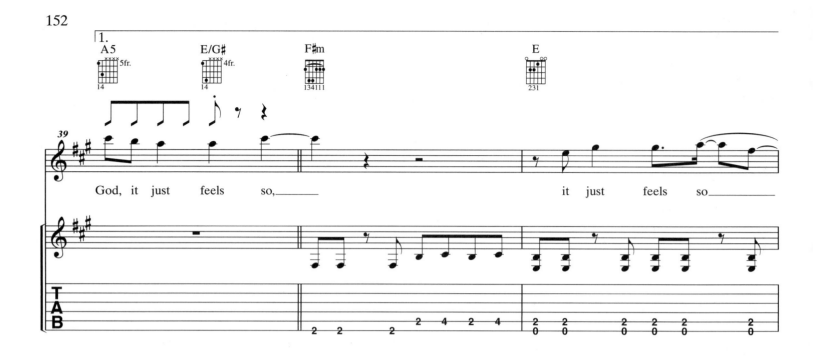

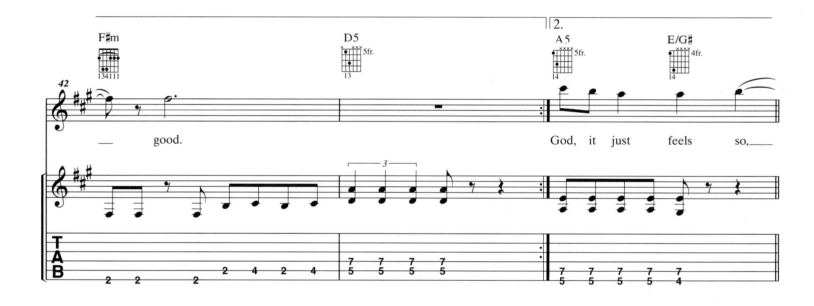

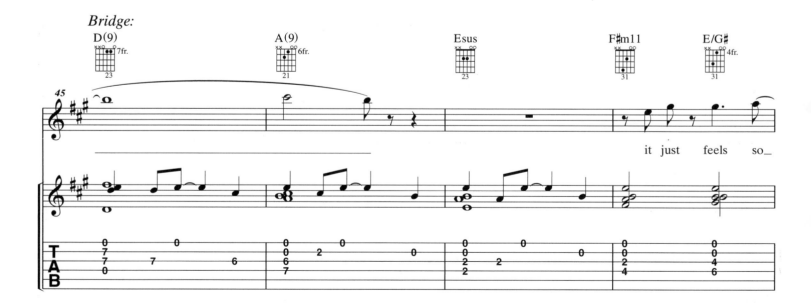

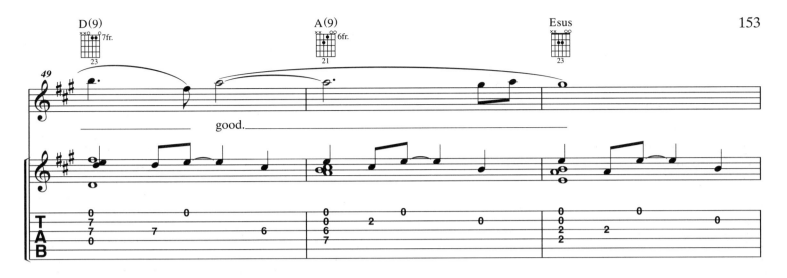

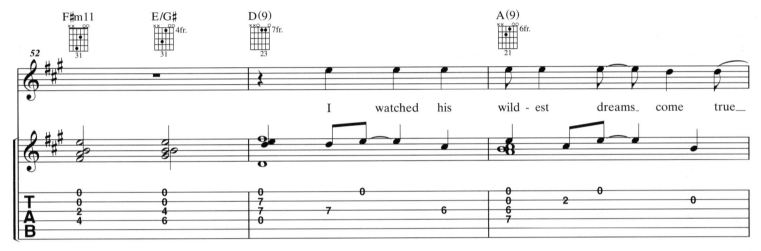

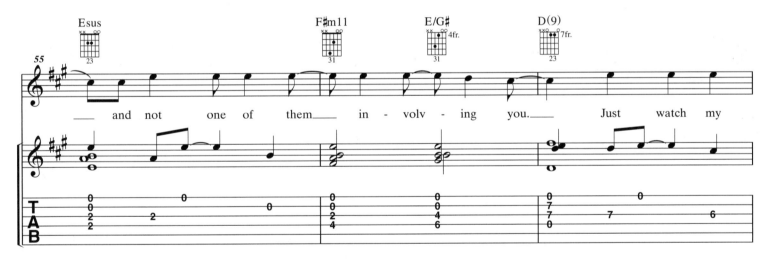

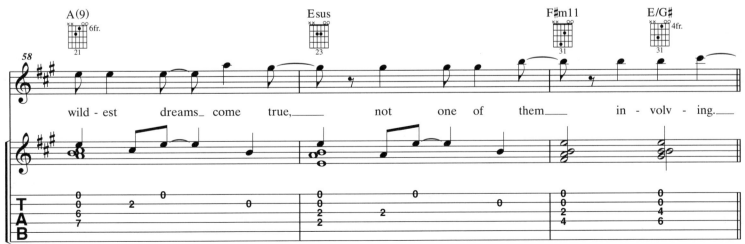

Guitar Solo:

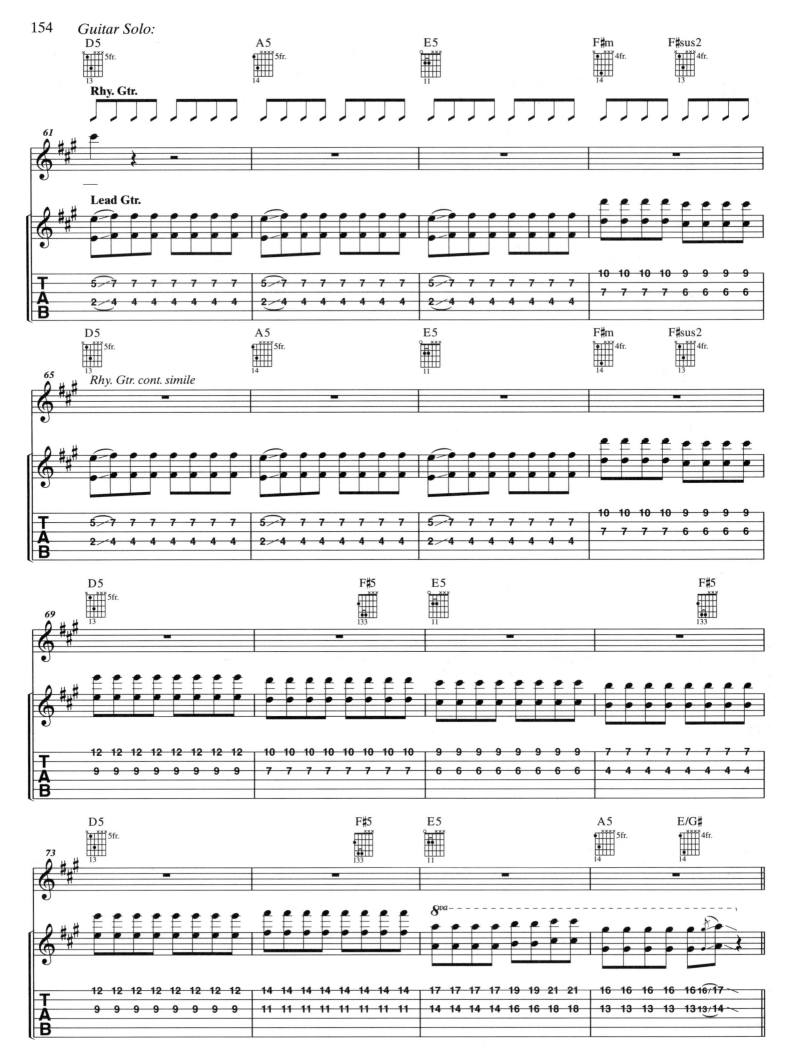

ONE

(as recorded by Three Dog Night)

Moderate shuffle ♩ = 126

Words and Music by
HARRY NILSSON

Verse 1:

One is the lone-li-est num-ber that you'll ev-er do.___

Two___ can be as bad as___ one;___ it's the lone-li-est num-ber since the num-ber o...   ...ne___

Elec. Gtr. *(w/dist.)*
8*va throughout*

One - 5 - 1

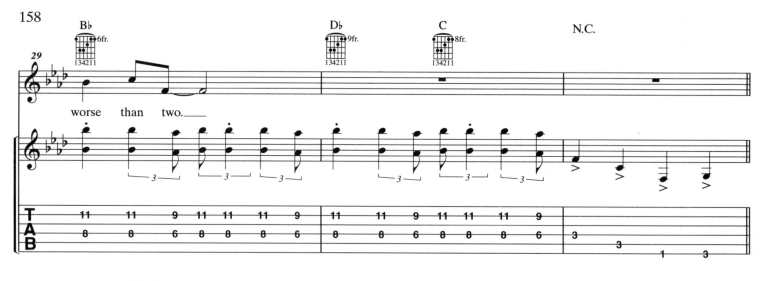

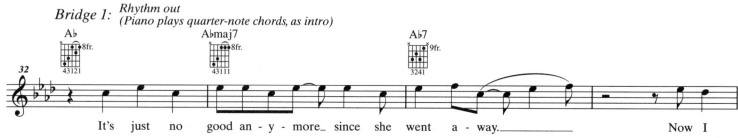

Bridge 1: **Rhythm out**
(Piano plays quarter-note chords, as intro)

It's just no good an-y-more_ since she went a-way.___ Now I

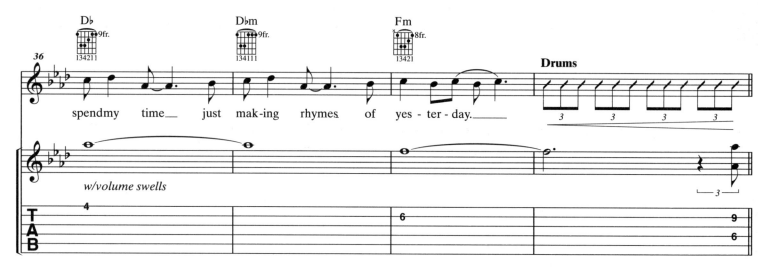

spend my time_ just mak-ing rhymes of yes-ter-day.___

Chorus:
w/Rhy. Fig. 1 *(Elec. Gtr.) cont. simile, 2 times*

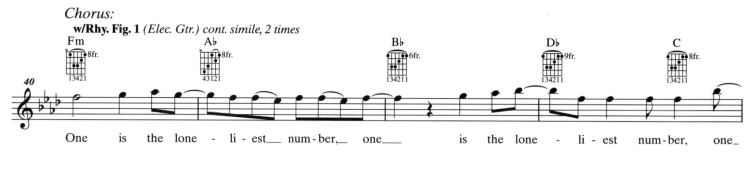

One is the lone-li-est_ num-ber,_ one_ is the lone-li-est num-ber, one_

_ is the lone-li-est num-ber that you'll ev-er do.__

One - 5 - 4

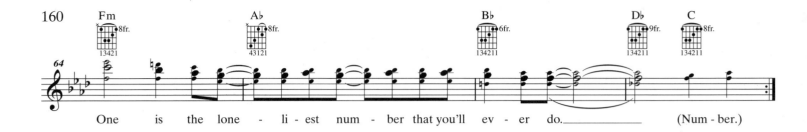

One   is   the   lone - li - est   num - ber that you'll   ev - er   do._____   (Num - ber.)

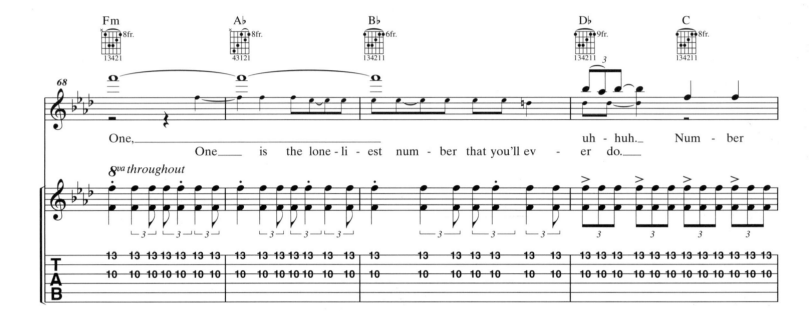

One,_____   _____   uh - huh.__   Num - ber
One____   is   the   lone - li - est   num - ber that you'll ev   -   er   do.__

8va throughout

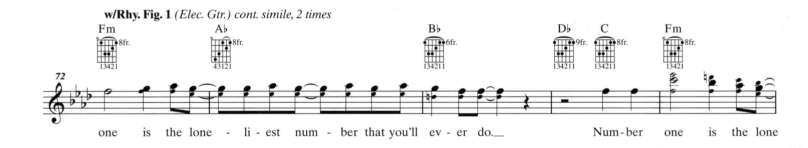

w/Rhy. Fig. 1 *(Elec. Gtr.) cont. simile, 2 times*

one   is   the   lone - li - est   num - ber that you'll   ev - er   do.__   Num - ber   one   is   the   lone

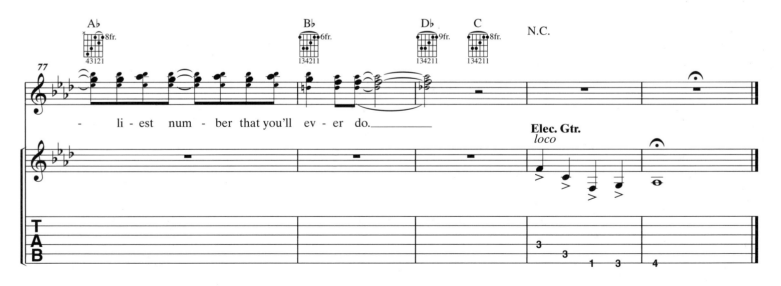

- li - est   num - ber that you'll   ev - er   do._____

Elec. Gtr.
loco

ONLY THE LONELY

Words and Music by
MARTHA DAVIS

Chorus:

told_____ you,   on - ly the lone - ly can   play.__   2. So

(2nd time only)

hold - - - - - - - ⌐

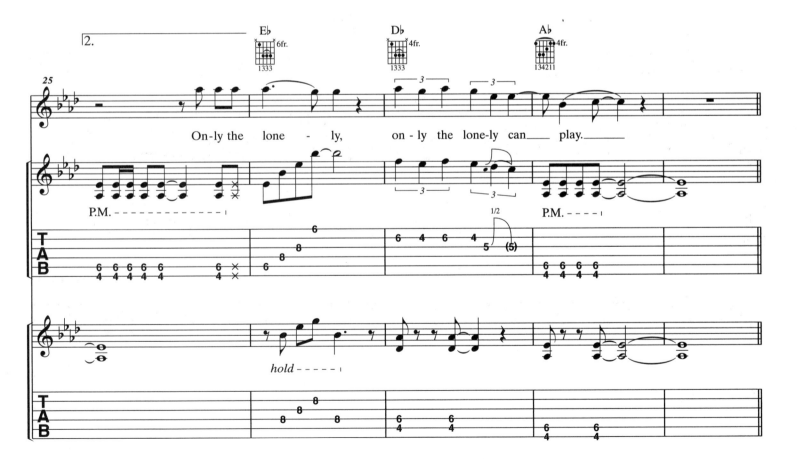

On-ly the lone - - ly,   on - ly the lone-ly can___ play._____

hold - - - - - ⌐

Guitar Solo:
w/Rhy. Fig. 2 *(Elec. Gtr. 2)*

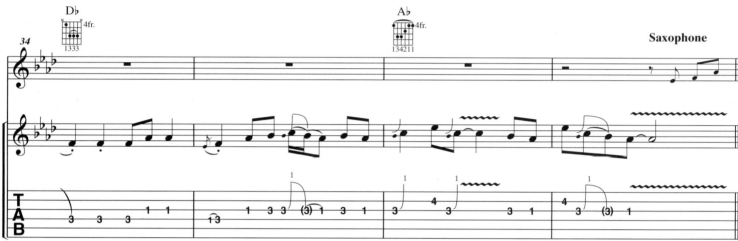

Saxophone Solo:
w/Rhy. Figs. 1 *(Elec. Gtr. 1)* **& 2** *(Elec. Gtr. 2)*

Chorus:

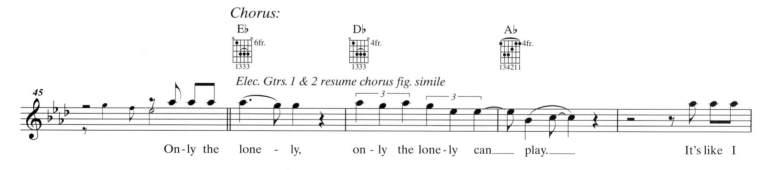

On - ly the lone - ly, on - ly the lone - ly can____ play.____ It's like I

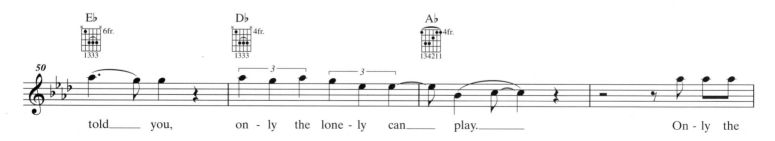

told____ you, on - ly the lone - ly can____ play._____ On - ly the

OPEN ARMS

Moderately slow ♩ = 104

Words and Music by
STEVE PERRY and JONATHAN CAIN

Intro:

Piano (arr. for gtr.)

fingerstyle

Verse:

Cont. rhy. simile

1. Ly - ing_____ be - side_____ you, here in_____ the dark;
2. Liv - ing_____ with - out_____ you; liv - ing_____ a - lone,

feel - ing your heart beat with mine.
this emp - ty house seems so cold.

Soft - ly_____ you whis - per, you're so_____ sin - cere.
Want - ing_____ to hold you, want - ing_____ you near;

Open Arms - 3 - 1

PARALYZER

Music and Lyrics by
SCOTT ANDERSON, Sean ANDERSON,
RICH BEDDOE, JAMES BLACK and RICK JACKETT

Paralyzer - 7 - 1

Verse:

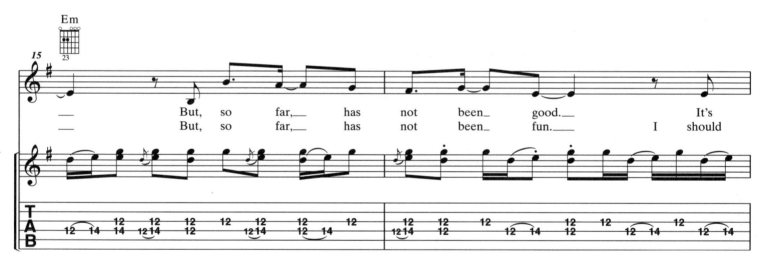

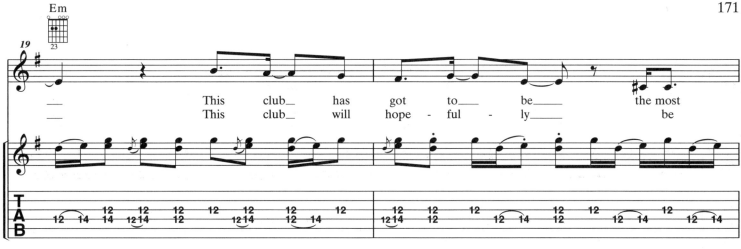

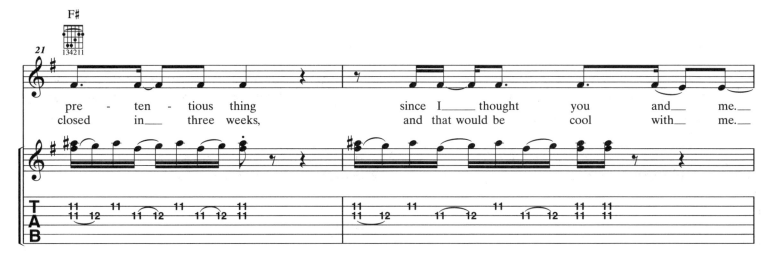

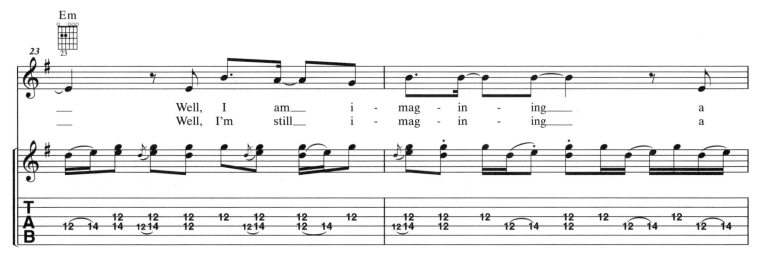

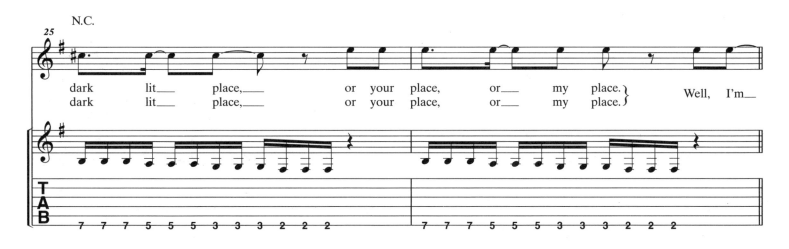

Chorus:

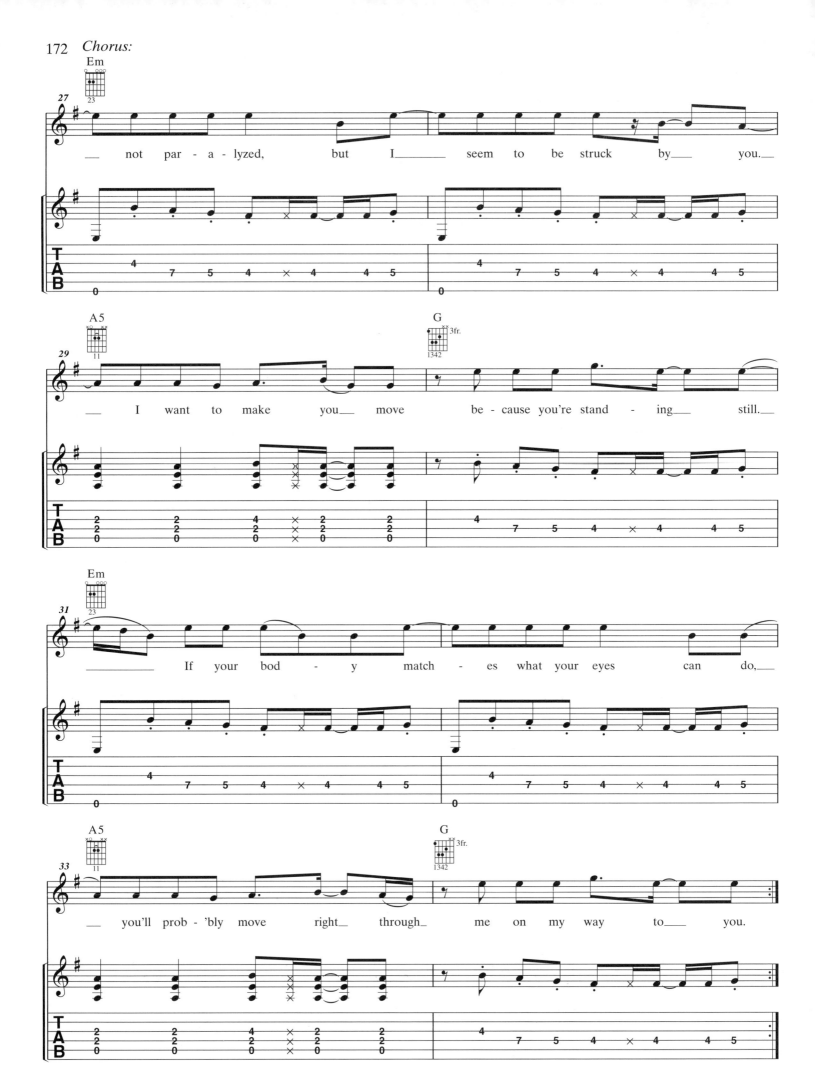

PARANOID ANDROID

Words and Music by
THOMAS YORKE, EDWARD O'BRIEN,
COLIN GREENWOOD, JONATHAN GREENWOOD
and PHILIP SELWAY

Verses 1 & 2:

1. Please, could you stop the noise I'm try'n' to get some rest,
2. When I am king you will be first a - gainst the wall,

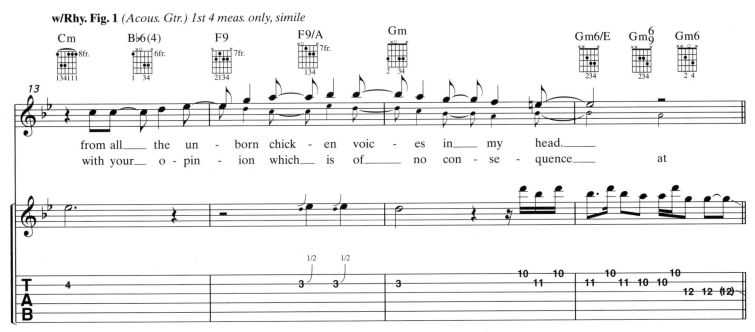

from all the un - born chick - en voic - es in my head.
with your o - pin - ion which is of no con - se - quence at

Chorus:

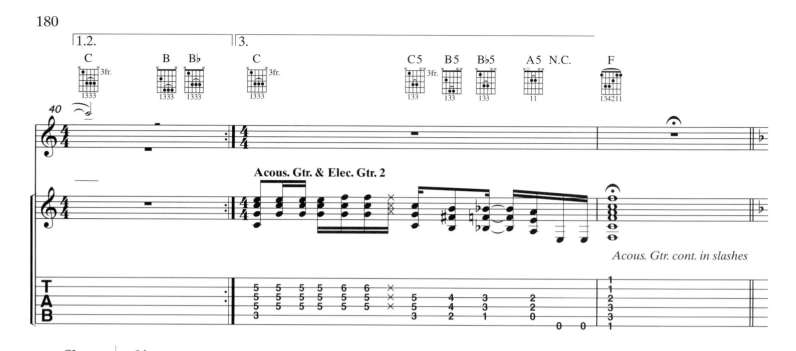

(What's So Funny 'Bout)
PEACE LOVE AND UNDERSTANDING

Words and Music by
NICK LOWE

(What's So Funny 'bout) Peace Love and Understanding - 2 - 1

(What's So Funny 'bout) Peace Love and Understanding - 2 - 2

PHOTOGRAPH

Tune down ½ step to match recording:

⑥ = E♭   ③ = G♭
⑤ = A♭   ② = B♭
④ = D♭   ① = E♭

Lyrics by CHAD KROEGER
Music by NICKELBACK

RUNNIN' WITH THE DEVIL

*To match record key, tune guitar down one half step.

Words and Music by
EDWARD VAN HALEN, ALEX VAN HALEN,
MICHAEL ANTHONY and DAVID LEE ROTH

Runnin' with the Devil - 3 - 1

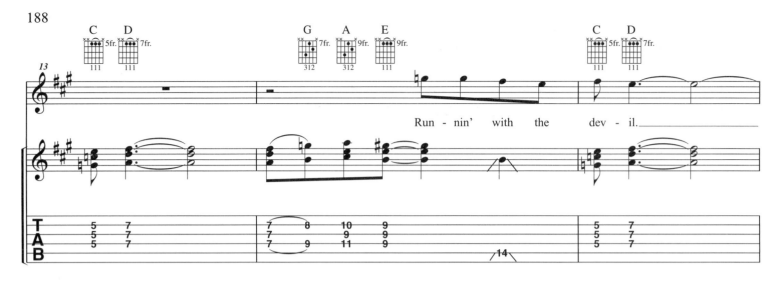

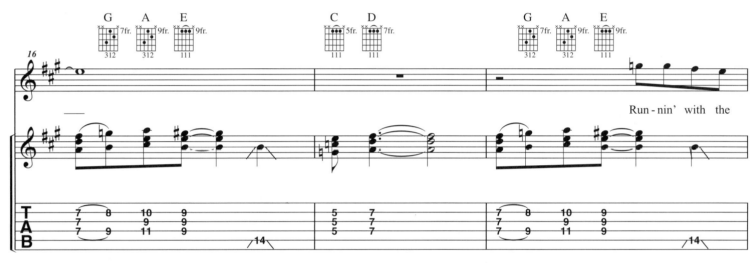

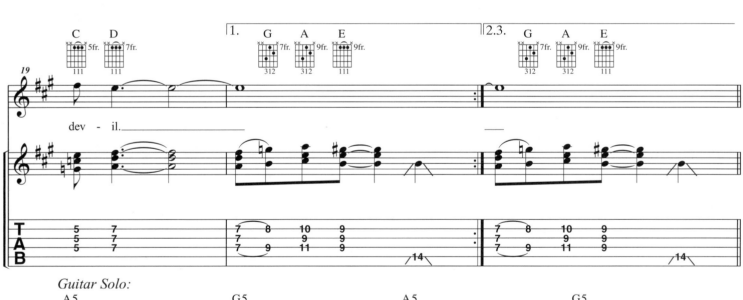

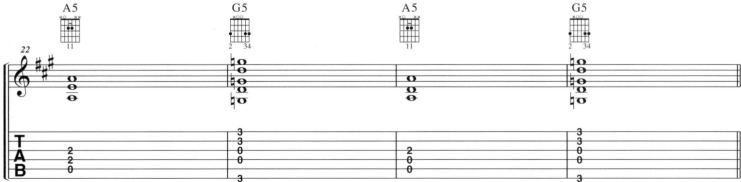

Verse 2:
I found the simple life ain't so simple
When I jumped out on that road.
I got no love, no love you'd call real.
Ain't got nobody waiting at home.
(To Chorus:)

Verse 3:
I found the simple life weren't so simple, no
When I jumped out on that road.
Got no love, no love you'd call real.
Got nobody waiting at home.
(To Chorus:)

RADIO FREE EUROPE

Words and Music by
WILLIAM BERRY, PETER BUCK,
MICHAEL MILLS and MICHAEL STIPE

THE REASON

Words and Music by
DANIEL ESTRIN and
DOUGLAS ROBB

The Reason - 4 - 1

The Reason - 4 - 4

RUNNING AWAY

Tune to Drop D:
⑥ = D   ③ = G
⑤ = A   ② = B
④ = D   ① = E

Music by DAN ESTRIN
Lyrics by DOUG ROBB

Moderately fast ♩ = 132
Intro:

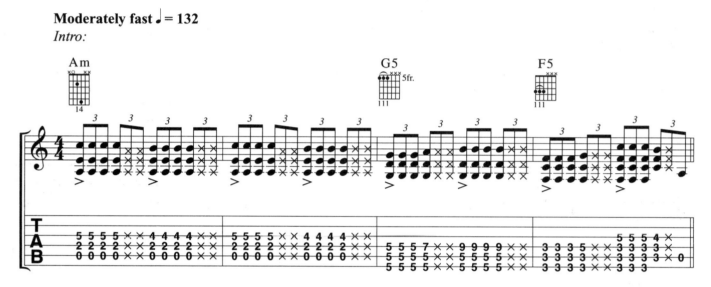

Verse:

1. I don't want you to give it all up and leave your own
2. I did e-nough to show you that I was will-ing to

life col-lect-ing dust. And I don't want you to feel sor-ry for____
give and sac-ri-fice. And I was the one who was lift-ing you____

1.
To Next Strain

2.

me, you nev-er gave us a chance to up when you thought your

Running Away - 3 - 1

SHOOTING STAR

Words and Music by
PAUL RODGERS

Shooting Star - 3 - 1

Verse 3:
Johnny made a record,
Went straight up to number one.
Suddenly everyone loved to hear him sing the song.
Watching the world go by,
Surprising it goes so fast.
Johnny looked around him and said,
"Well, I made the big name at last."
Don't you know?
Don't you know?
(To Chorus:)

Verse 4:
Johnny died one night,
Died in his bed.
Bottle of whiskey, sleeping tablets by his head.
Johnny's life passed him by
Like a warm summer day.
If you listen to the wind, you can
Still hear him play.
Oh, oh.
(To Chorus:)

RUNNING ON EMPTY

Words and Music by
JACKSON BROWNE

Running on Empty - 6 - 1

206

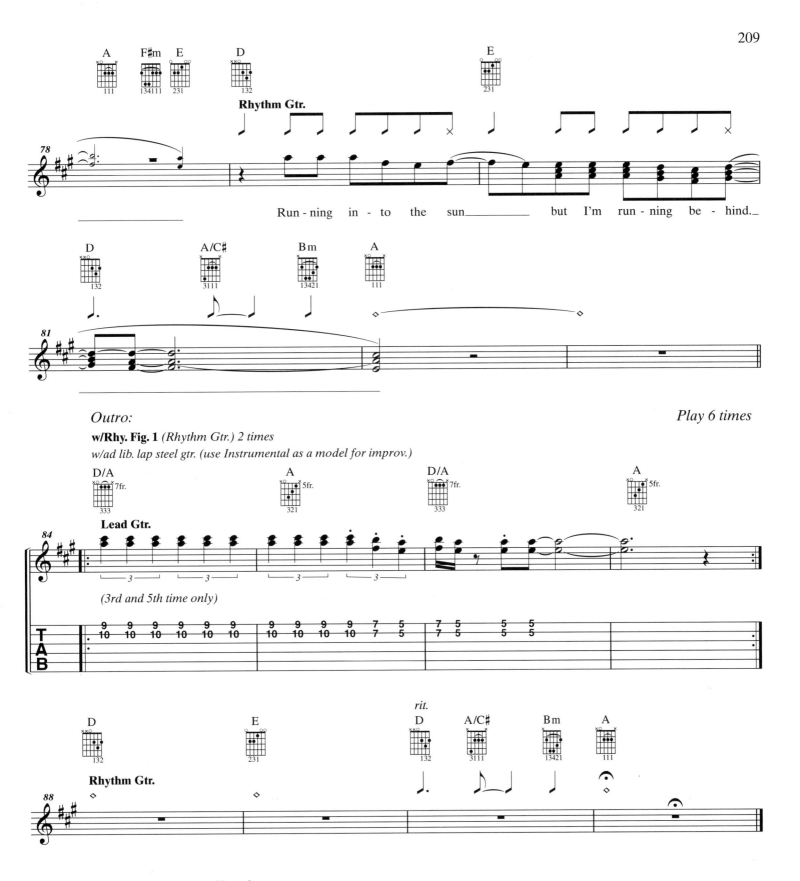

Run - ning in - to the sun_____ but I'm run - ning be - hind.__

Outro:

Play 6 times

w/Rhy. Fig. 1 *(Rhythm Gtr.) 2 times*

w/ad lib. lap steel gtr. (use Instrumental as a model for improv.)

Lead Gtr.

(3rd and 5th time only)

rit.

Rhythm Gtr.

Verse 2:
Gotta do what you can just to keep your love alive.
Tryin' not to confuse and with what you do to survive.
Sixty-nine, I was twenty-one, and I called the road my own.
I don't know when that road turned on to be the road I'm on.
(To Chorus:)

Verse 3:
Looking out at the road rushing under my wheels.
I don't know how to tell you all just how crazy this life feels.
I look around for the friends that I used to turn to, to pull me through.
Looking into their eyes, I see them running too.
(To Chorus:)

SEND THE PAIN BELOW

Music by
CHEVELLE
Words by
PETE LOEFFLER

Tune to Drop D:
⑥ = D ③ = G
⑤ = A ② = B
④ = D ① = E
To match recorded key, tune down 1½ steps

Moderate rock ♩ = 92
Intro:

*Recording sounds a minor 3rd lower than written.

Cont. in slashes

I_____ like hav-ing hurt.   So,

send the pain_ be - low   where I need_ it.   1. You used to

Verse:

Cont. rhy. simile

beg_____ me_ to take   care of things_____   and
run_____ me_ a - way   all while laugh - ing   then

Send the Pain Below - 4 - 1

*F♯ played by bass guitar only.

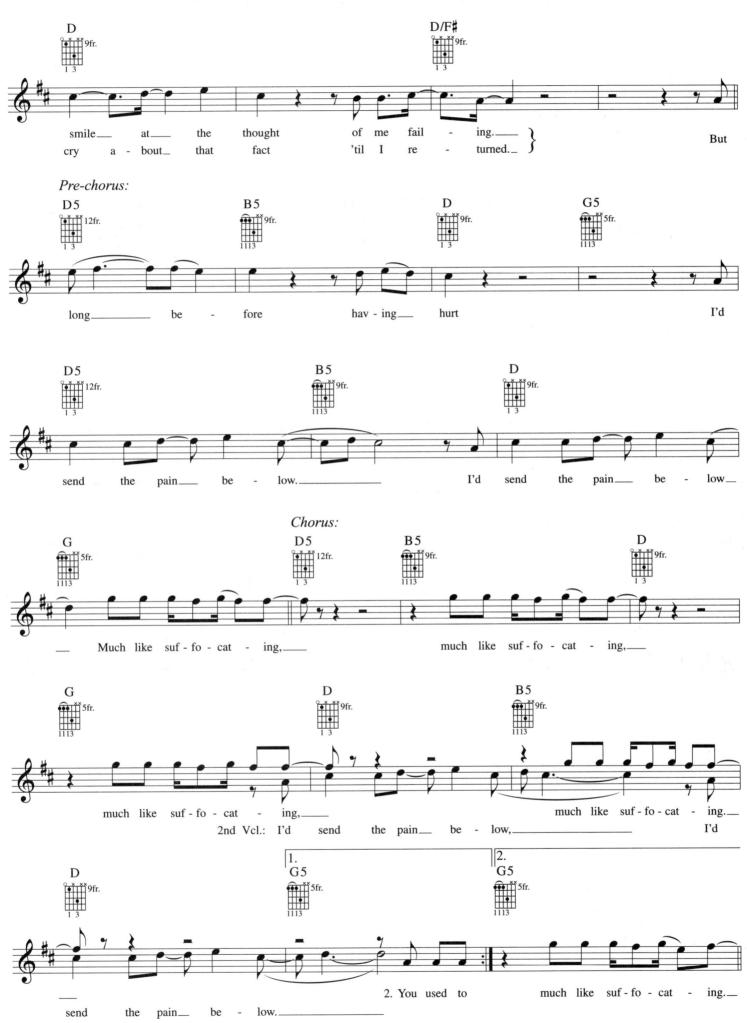

Bridge:

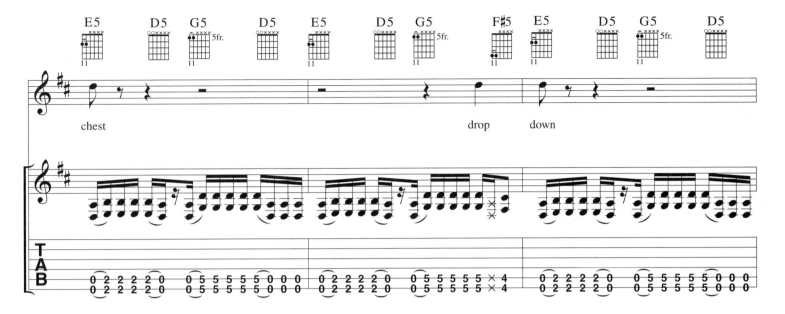

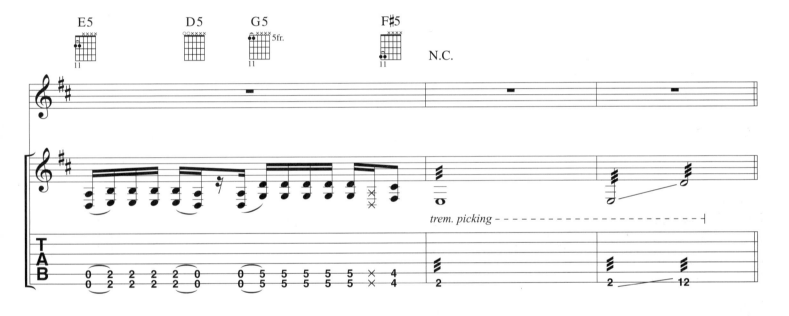

SHEENA IS A PUNK ROCKER

Words and Music by
JEFFREY HYMAN, JOHN CUMMINGS,
DOUGLAS COLVIN and THOMAS ERDELYI

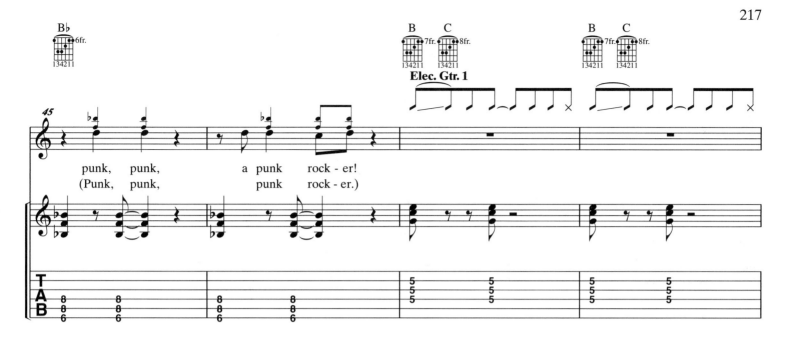

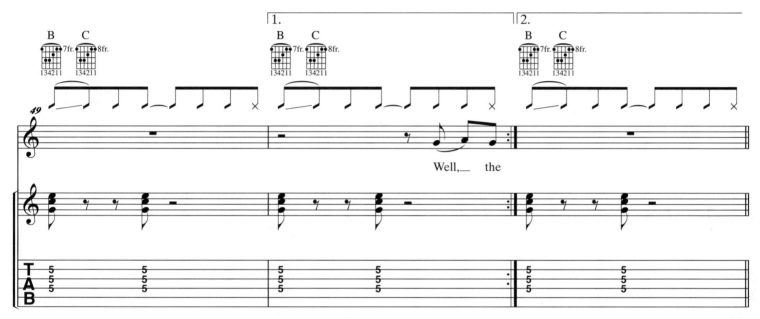

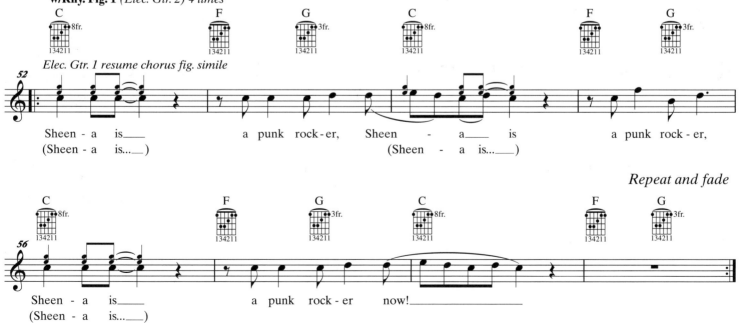

SMOOTH

Lyrics by
ROB THOMAS

Music by
ITAAL SHUR and ROB THOMAS

Smooth - 3 - 1

Smooth - 3 - 2

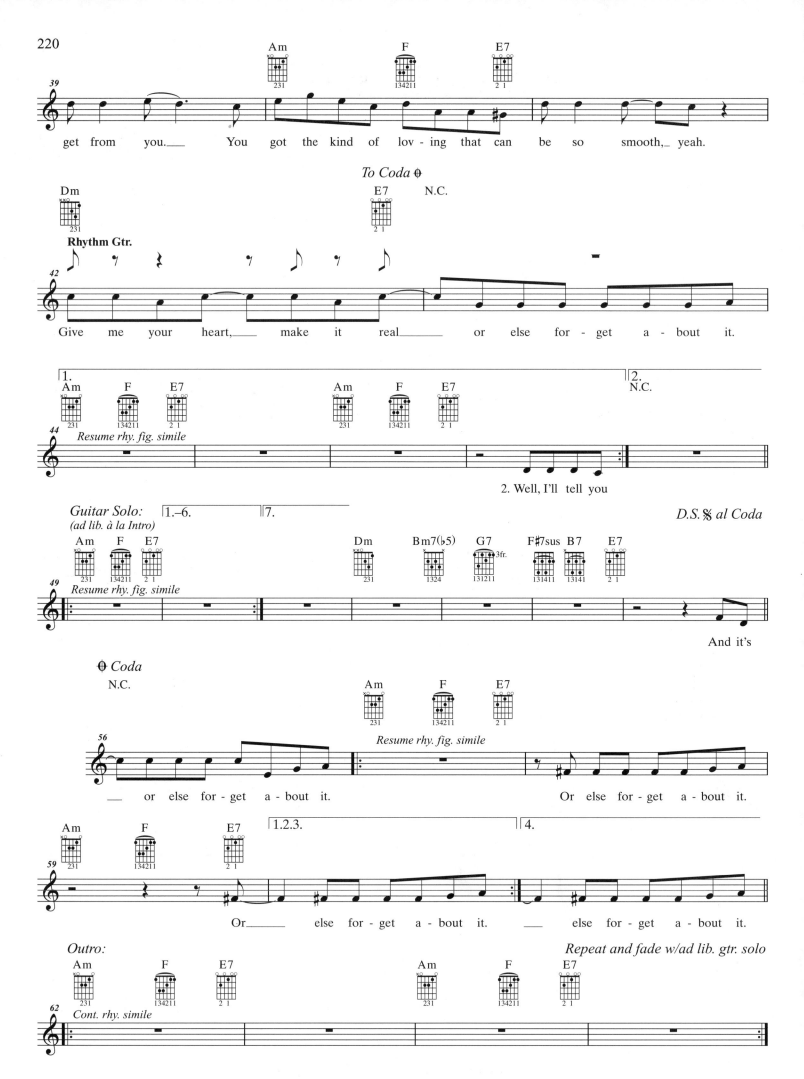

SO FAR AWAY

Music by
MIKE MUSHOK, AARON LEWIS,
JOHNNY APRIL and JON WYSOCKI
Lyrics by
AARON LEWIS

To match recorded key, tune down ½ step

Slowly ♩. = 45

1. This is my life, it's not what it was before. All these feelings I've shared and these are my

words that I've never said before. I think I'm doing okay and this is the

SOAK UP THE SUN

Words and Music by
SHERYL CROW
and JEFF TROTT

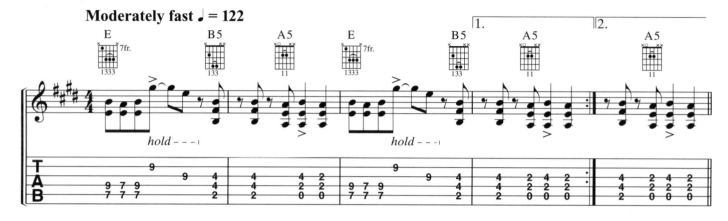

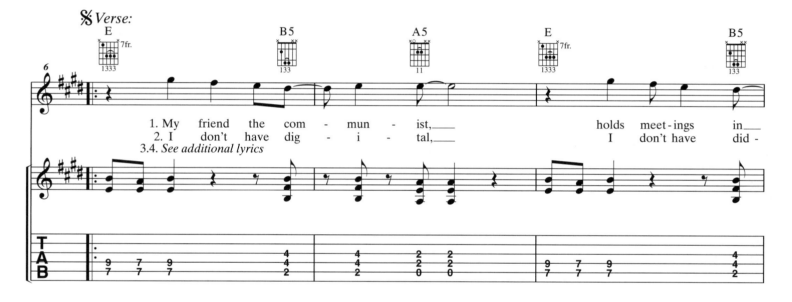

Soak Up the Sun - 6 - 1

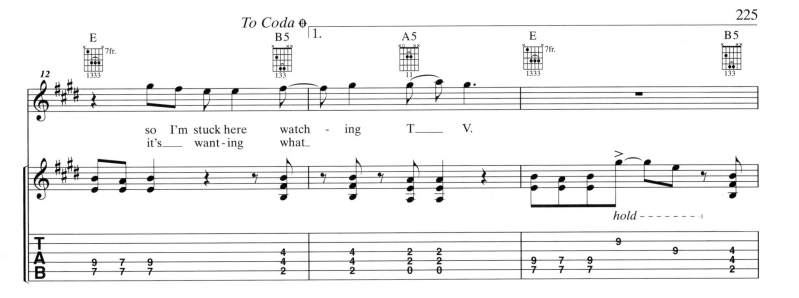

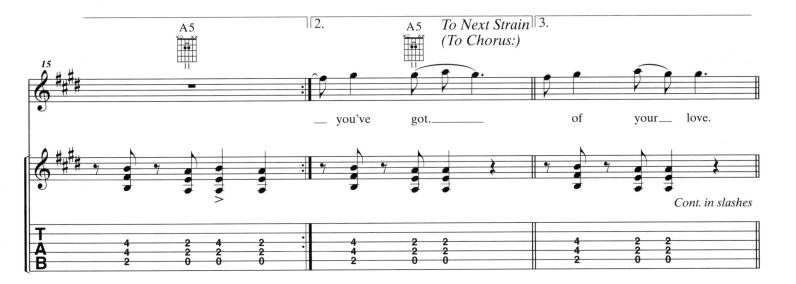

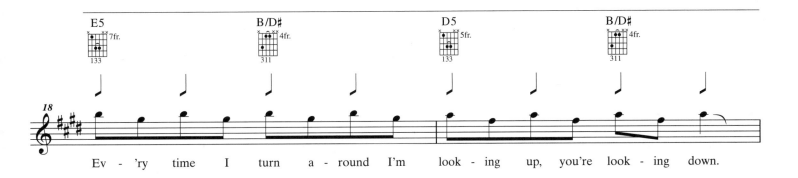

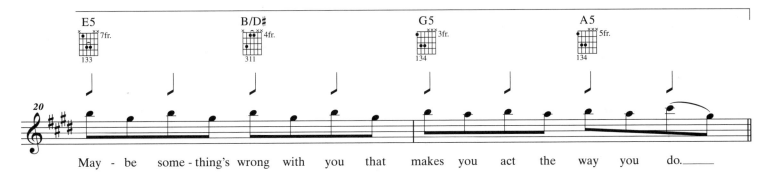

Soak Up the Sun - 6 - 2

Chorus:

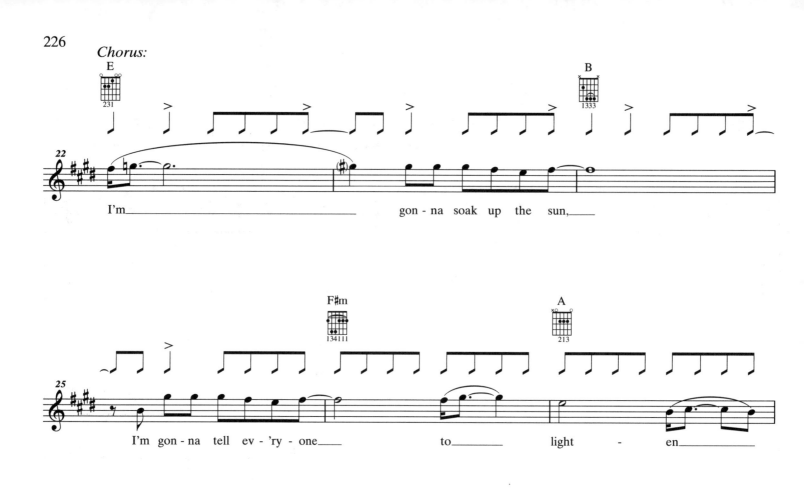

I'm_____ gon - na soak up the sun,_____

I'm gon - na tell ev - 'ry - one_____ to_____ light - en_____

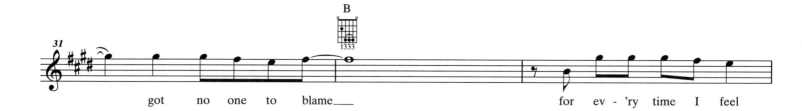

up._____ I'm gon - na tell 'em that I've_____

Cont. rhy. simile

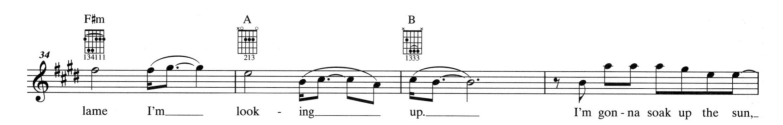

got no one to blame_____ for ev - 'ry time I feel

lame I'm_____ look - ing_____ up._____ I'm gon - na soak up the sun,_

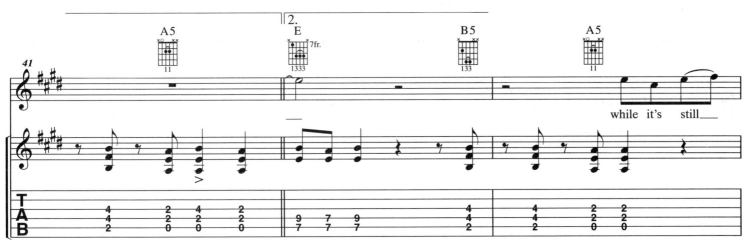

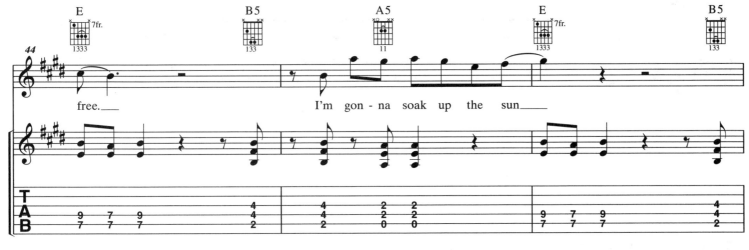

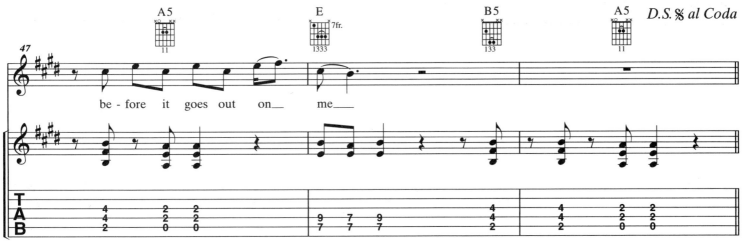

Soak Up the Sun - 6 - 4

Verse 3:
I've got a crummy job,
It don't pay near enough.
To buy the things it takes
To win me some of your love.
(To Bridge:)

Verse 4:
Don't have no master suite,
I'm still the king of me.
You have a fancy ride, but baby,
I'm the one who has the key.
(To Bridge:)

SORRY

Lyrics by
JOSH TODD
and MARTI FREDERIKSEN

Music by
JOSH TODD, KEITH NELSON
and MARTI FREDERIKSEN

Sorry - 4 - 1

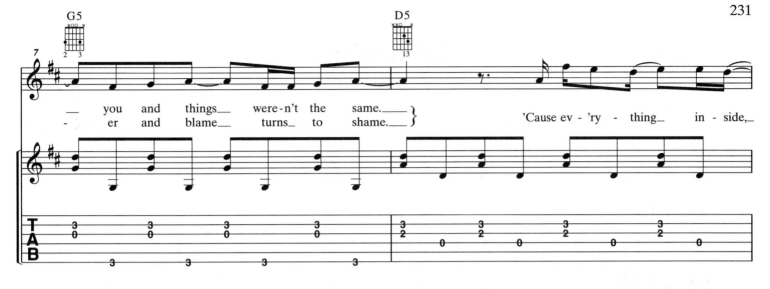

— you and things _were-n't the_ _same.___
- er and blame _turns_ _to_ _shame.___ }

'Cause ev - 'ry - thing_ in - side,_

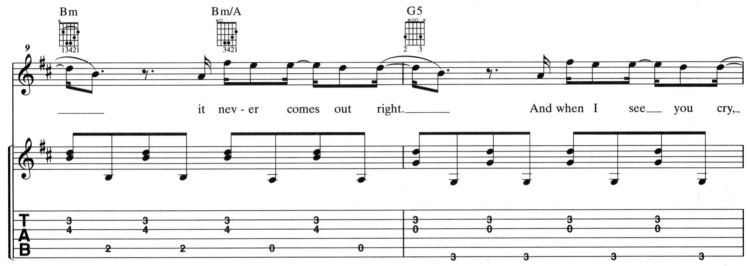

_____ it nev - er comes out right._____

And when I see_ you cry,_

_____ it makes me want_ to die._____

I'm sor - ry I'm bad,_

Cont. in slashes

Chorus:

Cont. rhy. simile

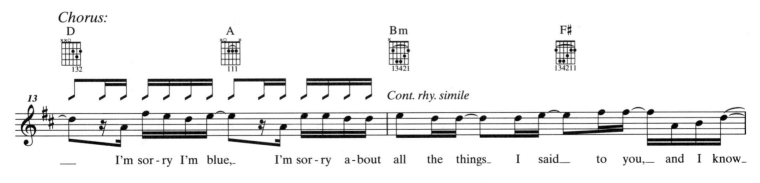

__ I'm sor - ry I'm blue,_ I'm sor - ry a-bout all the things_ I said_ to you,_ and I know_

SWEET CHILD O' MINE

Tune down ½ step to match recording:
⑥ = E♭   ③ = G♭
⑤ = A♭   ② = B♭
④ = D♭   ① = E♭

Words and Music by W. AXL ROSE, SLASH, IZZY STRADLIN,
DUFF McKAGAN and STEVEN ADLER

Moderately ♩ = 120

Intro:

Sweet Child o' Mine - 5 - 1

238

TOUCH OF GREY

Words by
ROBERT HUNTER
Music by
JERRY GARCIA

Touch of Grey - 3 - 1

Verse 2:
I see you've got your list out.
Say your piece and get out.
Yes, I get the gist of it, but it's all right.
Sorry that you feel that way.
The only thing there is to say:
Every silver lining's got a touch of grey.
(To Chorus:)

Bridge 2:
It's a lesson to me.
The Deltas and the East and the Freeze.
The ABC's we all think of,
To try to win a little love.

Verse 4:
I know the rent is in arrears,
The dog has not been fed in years.
It's even worse than it appears, but it's all right.
The cow is giving kerosene,
Kid can't read at seventeen.
The words he knows are all obscene, but it's all right.
(To Chorus:)

Verse 5:
The shoe is on the hand it fits.
There's really nothing much to it.
Whistle through your teeth and spit, 'cause it's all right.
Oh well, a touch of grey,
Kinda suits you anyway.
And that was all I had to say, and it's all right.
(To Chorus:)

Touch of Grey - 3 - 3

WHEN I COME AROUND

Lyrics by BILLIE JOE
Music by GREEN DAY

To match recorded key, tune down ½ step:

Moderately ♩ = 100

'cause you know__ where I'll be found   when I come a-round.__

Cont. rhy. simile

1.

2.

Cont. in notation

Ooh.

Guitar Solo:

Elec. Gtr. 2

Cont. in slashes

Chorus:

No   time   to   search   the   world   a - round

When I Come Around - 4 - 4

WHITE ROOM

Moderately ♩ = 114

Intro:

Words and Music by
JACK BRUCE and PETER BROWN

*Composite arrangement.

White Room - 5 - 1

*With ad lib. fills Verse 3.

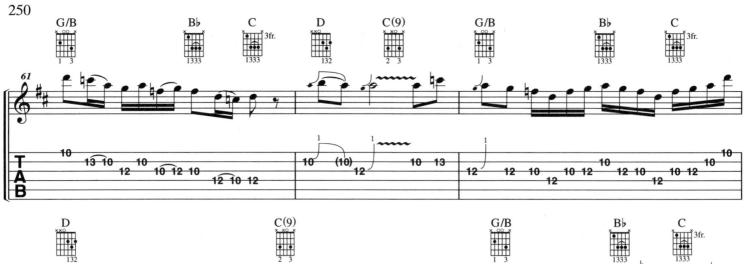

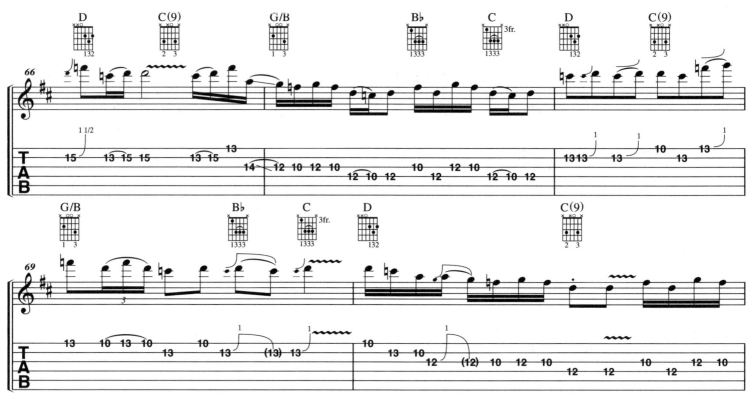

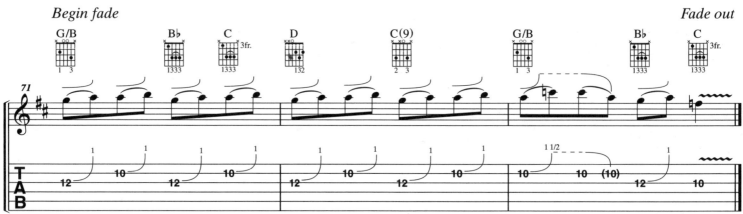

WITH ARMS WIDE OPEN

Gtr. tuned in Drop D:
⑥ = D ③ = G
⑤ = A ② = B
④ = D ① = E

Words and Music by
MARK TREMONTI and SCOTT STAPP

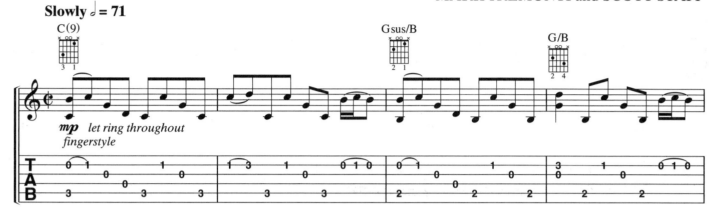

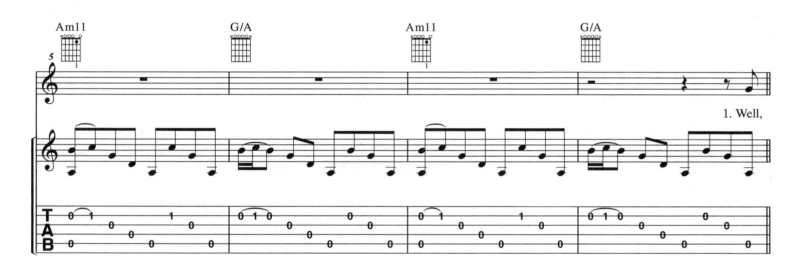

With Arms Wide Open - 5 - 1

to this place.___ I'll show you___ ev - 'ry - thing with arms_ wide

o - pen.___

With arms_ wide

o - pen.___

2. Well,

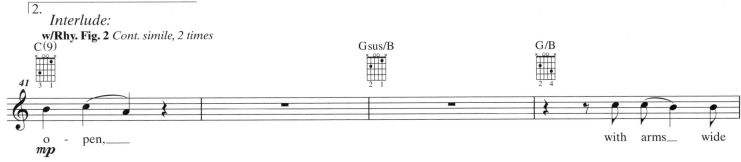

Interlude:
w/Rhy. Fig. 2 *Cont. simile, 2 times*

o - pen,___

with arms_ wide

GUITAR TAB GLOSSARY

TABLATURE EXPLANATION

TAB illustrates the six strings of the guitar.
Notes and chords are indicated by the placement of fret numbers on each string.

String ⑥, 3rd fret | String ①, 12th fret / String ③, 13th fret | A "C" chord | C chord arpeggiated

BENDING NOTES

Half Step:
Play the note and bend string one half step (one fret).

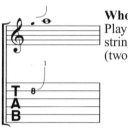

Whole Step:
Play the note and bend string one whole step (two frets).

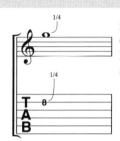

Slight Bend/ Quarter-Tone Bend:
Play the note and bend string sharp.

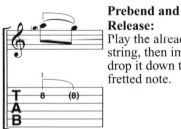

Prebend and Release:
Play the already-bent string, then immediately drop it down to the fretted note.

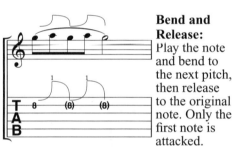

Bend and Release:
Play the note and bend to the next pitch, then release to the original note. Only the first note is attacked.

PICK DIRECTION

Downstrokes and Upstrokes:
The downstroke is indicated with this symbol (⊓) and the upstroke is indicated with this (∨).

ARTICULATIONS

Hammer On:
Play the lower note, then "hammer" your finger to the higher note. Only the first note is plucked.

Pull Off:
Play the higher note with your first finger already in position on the lower note. Pull your finger off the first note with a strong downward motion that plucks the string—sounding the lower note.

Palm Mute:
The notes are muted (muffled) by placing the palm of the pick hand lightly on the strings, just in front of the bridge.

Muted Strings:
A percussive sound is produced by striking the strings while laying the fret hand across them.

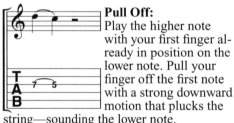

Legato Slide:
Play the first note and, keeping pressure applied on the string, slide up to the second note. The diagonal line shows that it is a slide and not a hammer-on or a pull-off.

HARMONICS

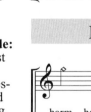

Natural Harmonic:
A finger of the fret hand lightly touches the string at the note indicated in the TAB and is plucked by the pick producing a bell-like sound called a harmonic.

RHYTHM SLASHES

Strum Marks/ Rhythm Slashes:
Strum with the indicated rhythm pattern. Strum marks can be located above the staff or within the staff.

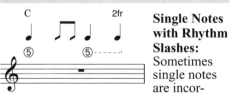

Single Notes with Rhythm Slashes:
Sometimes single notes are incorporated into a strum pattern. The circled number below is the string and the fret number is above.

Artificial Harmonic:
Fret the note at the first TAB number, lightly touch the string at the fret indicated in parens (usually 12 frets higher than the fretted note), then pluck the string with an available finger or your pick.